Discovering Literature Series

CHALLENGING LEVEL

Mockingjay

A Teaching Guide

by Mary Elizabeth

Community Strand

To Zippy.

GARLIC PRESS

Educational Materials for Teachers and Parents

899 South College Mall Road
Bloomington, IN 47401

www.garlicpress.com

In order to make it easy to use this teaching guide with digital and paperback versions, page numbers from *Catching Fire* for use in locating vocabulary words, quotations, and chapter beginnings match both the Kindle eBook and the Scholastic, Inc. paperback ISBN -13: 978-0-439-02353-5

Cover Art – Gale watching Katniss watch Peeta's first interview, pp 20–26
Chapter Art – Plutarch watching Katniss, who is seeing Cinna's sketchbook for the first time, p. 42
Strategy Page and Writer's Forum Art –Prim consoling Katniss in their room in District 13, p. 33

Publisher: Douglas M. Rife
Cover and interior illustrator: Ginny Joyner
Interior design: Mary Elizabeth
Cover design: Jenn Taylor

ISBN 978-1-930820-21-0
Order Number GP-207

Table of Contents

Table of Contents, cont.

Notes to the Teacher

The Discovering Literature Series is designed to develop students' appreciation for literature and to improve reading comprehension. The Challenging Level focuses on reading strategies that help students construct meaning as they read, as well as make connections between and among texts. The strategies taught in each guide reflect the demands of the particular literature selection, and material can be adapted or skipped to suit both class focus and students' developmental level, or even adapted for book club use.

Every teacher of literature faces a quandary in that the experience of literature—suspending one's disbelief and getting lost in the world of a story (aesthetic reading)—and the analysis of literature (efferent reading) cannot be carried on simultaneously. Thus, this guide is designed to be used with at least three different reading modes:

> • **Aesthetic/Analytic** Students read the book through first for the experience of the story (with or without vocabulary preparation) and use the guide afterwards to work on comprehension and analysis;

> • **Chapter-by-Chapter** Students read with limited preparation, but a thorough check-in on comprehension and analytic understanding after each chapter ensures comprehension is ongoing;

> • **Guided Reading** Students' reading is scaffolded with, for example, a purpose for reading each chapter (e.g., using Journal and Discussion questions that do not give away major plot elements), and following up as in the other modes.

CROSS-CURRICULAR LEARNING

Focused on political order and change and including a ballad, *Mockingjay* provides opportunities for lessons that could be fruitfully co-taught with a history teacher ("Justifying a Revolution," p. 23) or a music teacher ("Writing a Ballad," p. 31).

THE ELEMENTS IN THIS LITERATURE GUIDE

Reference to Book Page Numbers

To make it easier to teach students who have different editions, page numbers that match both paperback and Kindle editions are used to locate vocabulary words, quotations, and chapter beginnings. *HG, CF,* and *MJ* distinguish the three books.

Chapter Pages

Each Chapter Page is organized into three sections: **Chapter Vocabulary**, **Journal and Discussion Topics**, and a **Chapter Summary**.

The **Chapter Vocabulary** identifies challenging words and provides page numbers and definitions for the specific usage in the book. Introducing the **Chapter Vocabulary** prior to students' reading in any mode can help insure that their reading is not disrupted by unknown words, but since there may be a large amount of unfamiliar vocabulary, you may wish to do this over a period of time, not all at once. More interesting vocabulary activities will be possible if you treat multiple chapters' worth of vocabulary at once, and more meaningful vocabulary exercises will improve retention. A **Vocabulary–Word Study** feature, including suggested activities on vocabulary for the entire trilogy, is offered at the end of this guide (pp. 106–112). A master list may be downloaded from http://garlicpress.com/

If you do choose to present vocabulary by chapter, you could have students:

1. identify relationships between and among words, creating a web or other graphic that shows these relationships and adding related words.
2. look for multiple meaning words and synonyms (words that Collins uses in multiple, different meanings are marked "MM" in the vocabulary lists.)
3. use a set of words in a piece of writing, for example a poem, a personal anecdote, a one-act play, or a journal written in the persona of a character;

4. research the etymology of a set of vocabulary words;
5. make and exchange puzzles made with vocabulary words;
6. write and exchange cloze exercises using the vocabulary words;
7. identify subcategories of vocabulary, for example, words about war, verbs, words naming character attributes, five-syllable words, etc.

The **Journal and Discussion Topics** can be used as prompts for entries in students' Reading Response Journals if you choose to use them, as questions for discussion to help students become deeply engaged with the literature, and/or to check comprehension. If you wish to interact with students using their journals, the dialogue will be facilitated if you periodically collect the journals and respond to students' comments. It is important for students to know beforehand whether their journals are private or public. Even if they are public, many educators believe that journals should not be corrected or graded, but only check to be sure they are being used. You may also wish to keep your own journal.

Discussion can take place between partners, in small groups, or as a whole class. Students may also wish to reflect on the discussion in their journals. Discussion starters include:

1. review of predictions made for the chapter and whether they were accurate.
2. group retelling of the chapter in which everyone participates.
3. each group member sharing:
   a. the most striking moment in the chapter for him or her;
   b. a question she or he would like to ask the author or a character; or
   c. what he or she liked most or least about the chapter.
4. analysis of how the chapter relates to the preceding material.

The **Chapter Summary** for each chapter is included for teacher use only. While the name I've given to the chapter (Collins does not name her chapters) provides an at-a-glance review of the chapter, the summary has enough details to refresh your memory about specific contents of each chapter. The summaries should never be used to replace reading the work of literature. Note that while the suggested questions always include a summarization idea, these questions are couched so that the summaries provided in this book will not provide adequate answers.

Strategy Pages

Strategy Pages are developed to increase students' understanding of strategies they can use to enhance their understanding of literature. A strategic approach does not eschew the teaching of skills, but takes instruction farther by helping students understand how and when to deploy their skills, that is, choose appropriate skills to employ in various literary situations. Having a strategic understanding of how meaning is made by the interaction of authors' words and readers' understanding and imagination can lead to enriched reading experiences. *MJ* reviews most of the 45 strategies taught in the first two guides within Journal and Discussion questions and Tests and adds 13 more. Students will have the opportunity to consider topics such as Collins's use of a variety of tropes, how Collins combines elements of a number of genres, and a comparison of the Panem districts' justification for revolution with that outlined in the Declaration of Independence.

You may copy and distribute Strategy pages. Students can answer on the back of the page or on a separate sheet of paper. Some Strategy Page questions require ongoing attention as the students continue reading.

Tests

At the end of each of the three parts of the novel, a comprehensive **Test** has been provided for your use. Each test includes vocabulary exercises and short essay topics. You may copy and distribute these pages, which students may complete with or without access to the text, as you decide. You can also feel free to select from among the questions, rather than have students answer all of them.

Writer's Forum Pages

Each **Writer's Forum** page presents instruction about a particular genre or writing strategy and directions for a particular writing task. Assignments draw on both the literature and students' own experience of the text. You can choose from these suggestions or substitute your own creative-writing ideas. Besides the six Writer's Forums in this guide, there are plenty of writing opportunities that draw on the 17 types of writing introduced in the first two guides in the Journal and Discussion topics and the Tests, which could be developed into full lessons, if you wish.

As you plan writing lessons, allow enough time for students to engage in the writing process:

- **Prewrite** (brainstorm and plan their work)
- **Draft** (give a shape to their ideas on paper)
- **Review** (revisit their work with an eye to improving it, on their own as well as with peers, with you, or with other reviewers)
- **Revise** (make changes that they feel will improve their draft)
- **Proofread** (check for accuracy in grammar, mechanics, and spelling)
- **Publish** (present their work to others in some way)

Theme Pages

There are several different ways to approach theme, starting with Strategy Page: Identifying Themes (p. 64) and the Theme Page (p. 71). You can also set this work in the context of other works of literature that focus on community using our other literature guides in "The Community" series or other works with a community theme, for example, these dystopias:

- *Animal Farm* or *Nineteen Eighty-Four* by George Orwell
- *Brave New World* by Aldous Huxley
- *Ender's Game* by Orson Scott Card
- *Fahrenheit 451* by Ray Bradbury
- "Harrison Bergeron" by Kurt Vonnegut
- "The Lottery" by Shirley Jackson
- *The Time Machine* by H. G. Wells
- *V for Vendetta* by Alan Moore and David Lloyd

A group of books with similar themes can also throw light on Big Ideas. Big Ideas worth considering include the following:

- How can a person function without the ability to discern what is real/true?
- What does the community owe the individual and vice versa?
- How can individuals best respond when a community is or becomes unjust or otherwise damaging to individuals' interests?

Answer Pages

Possible responses are given in the **Answer Pages**. The responses include critical analysis of the novel that you may find useful. Students' answers are expected to be more developed than the sample answers in many cases.

TEACHING WITH DIGITAL EDITIONS

One of the advantages of many digital editions is the ready access to definitions of every word, but there are three reasons that it is not wise to rely on this in place of teaching vocabulary: 1) it interrupts the reader's experience of the story; 2) the definition offered may not match the use in the text; 3) the word may not appear (for example, Collins's neologisms). On the other hand, digital editions may allow adjustment of brightness, font, text size, and line length, giving the reader more control over the reading experience, and may also allow note-taking. The device may be able to read the book aloud, but you may wish to check the quality of this feature.

INTRODUCING THE LITERATURE

How you choose to introduce the literature will likely depend on the student and reading mode. For Aesthetic/Analytic reading, you may simply hand the student an edition and allow the author to unfold the world of the story in his or her own

Notes to the Teacher

way. To prepare students to read the work aesthetically, explain that in a work of fiction, an author creates an imaginary world. An important task in beginning a literature selection is coming to terms with that world.

When students need guidance and when you are teaching analysis, you can use this guide to help students contextualize *Mockingjay* using Strategy 1: Beginning the Final Book in a Series, p. 11). If your class is reading the entire trilogy, you may already know what familiarity students have with the series and author. If it seems appropriate, you may wish to correct any misapprehensions students have, e.g., conclusions drawn from the movies that don't fit the books. You may wish to specifically encourage students to—as much as they can—set aside what they know from outside sources and read the text on its own terms.

Whatever mode students are using, it is a good idea to point out that it is possible to consciously assess one's own understanding and that this process is called *metacognitive reflection*. Also point out that doing so may interrupt the experience of the story until such reflection becomes seamlessly integrated into the reader's process. You may wish to review the process by modeling with a think-aloud approach as you go through questions 3–5 in Strategy 1 (for aesthetic reading, skip over the others for now). Simply read aloud the portion of *Mockingjay* (or another book, if you don't want to influence students' reading) needed to answer the questions, and speak aloud your thoughts as you formulate your responses, making explicit the connections and prior knowledge you are developing in your thoughts. Continue with whichever prereading activities you have determined are appropriate.

Sample Lesson Plan

It's likely that students will eventually end up reading chapter-by-chapter. If they are using the aesthetic/analytic approach, this will be their second reading of the book. At this point, all students can engage in prereading, during reading, and after reading activities geared for their abilities and needs.

Prereading Activities: Choose these activities based on how much prereading guidance students need and what can be handled after they read. Prereading activities may include:

- previewing vocabulary and doing a vocabulary exercise;
- reviewing the developments of the previous chapter(s); and
- reviewing predictions.

During Reading: Students can read with their Reading Journals handy, if it suits their reading mode: if they are experiencing the story and don't want to be interrupted to do a journal entry, allow them to write in the journal after they read. If students need guidance as they read, you may wish to give them some of the journal and discussion topics before they read to help focus their attention. Additional journal activities they can use with every chapter include the following:

- recording questions they have about what they have read;
- recording associations they have made between this text and other texts, experiences, or situations; and
- taking notes on the images and/or feelings the text evoked.

After Reading: Students can complete the Journal and Discussion Topics, and the Writer's Forum and Strategy Pages and Test (if any). You may wish to end each discussion by having students explain and note their predictions

SUZANNE COLLINS AND THE HUNGER GAMES TRILOGY

Collins was born in Connecticut in 1962, but the fact that her father was in the military meant that her childhood was spent at a number of locations in the U.S. and overseas. A military historian, her father shared his understandings of the world with his children, so Collins grew up with an awareness of war. After spending a number of years writing for children's television shows, she met James Proimos, an author of children's books, who inspired her and to whom *The Hunger Games* is dedicated. Her fantasy series *The Underland Chronicles* was published between 2003 and 2007 and treats war in a variety of ways. The Hunger Games trilogy, the first novel of which was published in 2008, progresses from a war game in the first book, to a revolution in the second, and a war in the third.

The story of *The Hunger Games* sprang from several roots. Collins—a fan of Greek mythology—was influenced by the story of King Minos of Crete imposing a yearly tribute of seven youths and seven maidens on Athens, and thrusting them into the labyrinth, where they were slain by the Minotaur. until Theseus intervened. Collins identified slave, gladiator, and warrior Spartacus as an inspiration for the overall shape of the series (see p. 62 for a lesson on Collins's influences). Collins was also inspired by an incident of channel surfing in which she alternated between a reality TV program and real war coverage until the two began to blend in her mind.

THE HUNGER GAMES MOVIES

Collins contributed to the screenplays for the movie version of *The Hunger Games* (2012), and the differences between the books and the movies are likely to come up as you teach the novel. Collins herself pointed to three important differences in an interview with Scholastic, and although she was talking about the first movie, these concerns extend to the others:

> **Q: We understand you worked on the initial screenplay for a film to be based on *The Hunger Games* What is the biggest difference between writing a novel and writing a screenplay?**
>
> A: There were several significant differences. Time, for starters. When you're adapting a novel into a two-hour movie you can't take everything with you. The story has to be condensed to fit the new form. Then there's the question of how best to take a book told in the first person and present tense and transform it into a satisfying dramatic experience. In the novel, you never leave Katniss for a second and are privy to all of her thoughts so you need a way to dramatize her inner world and to make it possible for other characters to exist outside of her company. Finally, there's the challenge of how to present the violence while still maintaining a PG-13 rating so that your core audience can view it. A lot of things are acceptable on a page that wouldn't be on a screen. But how certain moments are depicted will ultimately be in the director's hands.
>
> (http://www.scholastic.com/thehungergames/media/suzanne_collins_q_and_q. pdf)

So, students who have seen the movies and try to avoid reading the books are likely to make mistakes in point of view, leaving out details, and providing different descriptions of the violence. As of this writing, the two-part movie version of *Mockingjay* has not been released, but we can assume that—like the first two movies—they will not maintain the first-person point of view of Katniss and will include material that Katniss is not party to. One way to dispel the movie's influence is to help students analyze the movie so thoroughly that they gain a detailed understanding of how (and why) it differs from the book: this makes it much easier to keep the two separate.

THE COMMON CORE STATE STANDARDS INITIATIVE

The Common Core State Standards Initiative proposes educational standards that aim to "provide a consistent, clear understanding of what students are expected to learn, so teachers and parents know what they need to do to help them." As of October 2013, 45 states and four US territories have adopted the Common Core Standards. The following chart shows how exercises and activities in this teaching guide align with the relevant Common Core standards. Because this guide may be used across a range of ages and grade levels, the chart refers to the key content of each standard across grades 6–12.

The Common Core Standards emphasize skills and knowledge, so you may wonder why this teaching guide emphasizes *strategies* and how strategies and skills are related. A *strategy* is the knowledge of when and how to deploy your skills for the most effective results. If you have skills and don't know when and how to use them, they don't do much good. The strategy lessons in this teaching guide provide instruction in skills, contextualized with information about when and how to use them effectively.

Common Core
Correlation

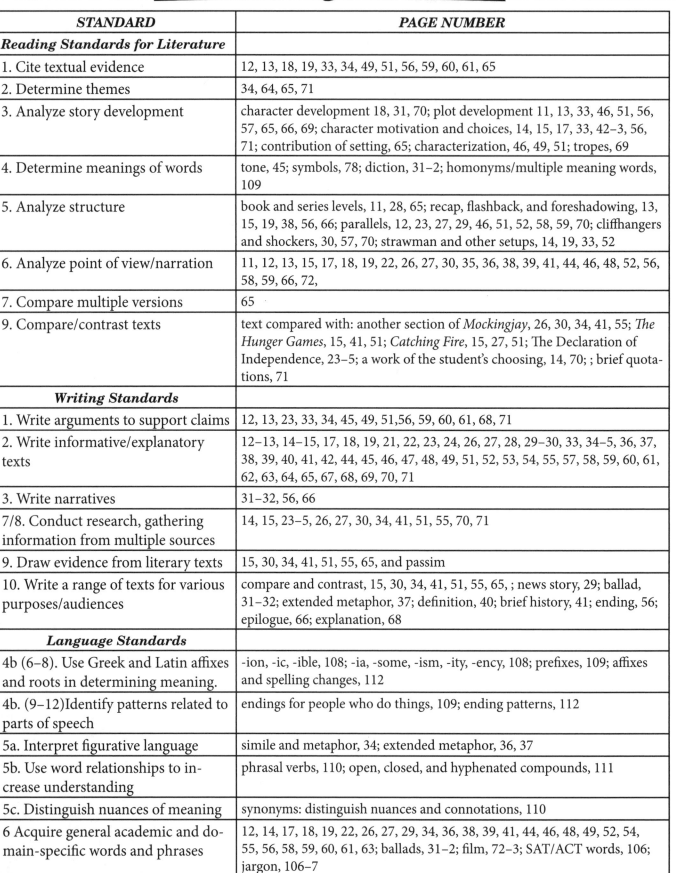

STANDARD	PAGE NUMBER
Reading Standards for Literature	
1. Cite textual evidence	12, 13, 18, 19, 33, 34, 49, 51, 56, 59, 60, 61, 65
2. Determine themes	34, 64, 65, 71
3. Analyze story development	character development 18, 31, 70; plot development 11, 13, 33, 46, 51, 56, 57, 65, 66, 69; character motivation and choices, 14, 15, 17, 33, 42–3, 56, 71; contribution of setting, 65; characterization, 46, 49, 51; tropes, 69
4. Determine meanings of words	tone, 45; symbols, 78; diction, 31–2; homonyms/multiple meaning words, 109
5. Analyze structure	book and series levels, 11, 28, 65; recap, flashback, and foreshadowing, 13, 15, 19, 38, 56, 66; parallels, 12, 23, 27, 29, 46, 51, 52, 58, 59, 70; cliffhangers and shockers, 30, 57, 70; strawman and other setups, 14, 19, 33, 52
6. Analyze point of view/narration	11, 12, 13, 15, 17, 18, 19, 22, 26, 27, 30, 35, 36, 38, 39, 41, 44, 46, 48, 52, 56, 58, 59, 66, 72,
7. Compare multiple versions	65
9. Compare/contrast texts	text compared with: another section of *Mockingjay*, 26, 30, 34, 41, 55; *The Hunger Games*, 15, 41, 51; *Catching Fire*, 15, 27, 51; The Declaration of Independence, 23–5; a work of the student's choosing, 14, 70; ; brief quotations, 71
Writing Standards	
1. Write arguments to support claims	12, 13, 23, 33, 34, 45, 49, 51,56, 59, 60, 61, 68, 71
2. Write informative/explanatory texts	12–13, 14–15, 17, 18, 19, 21, 22, 23, 24, 26, 27, 28, 29–30, 33, 34–5, 36, 37, 38, 39, 40, 41, 42, 44, 45, 46, 47, 48, 49, 51, 52, 53, 54, 55, 57, 58, 59, 60, 61, 62, 63, 64, 65, 67, 68, 69, 70, 71
3. Write narratives	31–32, 56, 66
7/8. Conduct research, gathering information from multiple sources	14, 15, 23–5, 26, 27, 30, 34, 41, 51, 55, 70, 71
9. Draw evidence from literary texts	15, 30, 34, 41, 51, 55, 65, and passim
10. Write a range of texts for various purposes/audiences	compare and contrast, 15, 30, 34, 41, 51, 55, 65, ; news story, 29; ballad, 31–32; extended metaphor, 37; definition, 40; brief history, 41; ending, 56; epilogue, 66; explanation, 68
Language Standards	
4b (6–8). Use Greek and Latin affixes and roots in determining meaning.	-ion, -ic, -ible, 108; -ia, -some, -ism, -ity, -ency, 108; prefixes, 109; affixes and spelling changes, 112
4b. (9–12)Identify patterns related to parts of speech	endings for people who do things, 109; ending patterns, 112
5a. Interpret figurative language	simile and metaphor, 34; extended metaphor, 36, 37
5b. Use word relationships to increase understanding	phrasal verbs, 110; open, closed, and hyphenated compounds, 111
5c. Distinguish nuances of meaning	synonyms: distinguish nuances and connotations, 110
6 Acquire general academic and domain-specific words and phrases	12, 14, 17, 18, 19, 22, 26, 27, 29, 34, 36, 38, 39, 41, 44, 46, 48, 49, 52, 54, 55, 56, 58, 59, 60, 61, 63; ballads, 31–2; film, 72–3; SAT/ACT words, 106; jargon, 106–7

Strategy 1

Plot—Beginning the Final Book in a Trilogy

Directions:
First, read the information. Then, answer the question or questions.

Beginning the final book in a series has its own particular demands. On the one hand, you have prior knowledge from the earlier books (and maybe other books by the same author, as well). You know the genre and a good deal about the world of the book, the characters, the themes, the narrator, and more. You may have explicit knowledge about some of the plot developments that are coming up, or at least some pretty shrewd guesses.

But two types of problems can arise right off the bat when you start the final book in a series. It may have been a while since you read the earlier books, so the author's references to them may slip by you. Or you may have seen a movie or game version that has melded with your memory of the books, so that you're not quite sure which is which in some cases. These issues are fairly simple to address if you have the time to reread the earlier books before beginning the final one. And while you're rereading, you may even identify some patterns or themes that weren't clear to you previously.

There's another aspect of beginning a final book and that is its place in the whole. We know—from Collins background as a television writer, her discussion of plot in interviews, and simply by looking at the division of the series and each book—that Collins structured her work with reference to a three-act structure. This means that each book has two levels of plot: it works as a three-act structure in itself, and it works as an act of the larger three-act structure of the trilogy, making *Mockingjay* function as Act Three.

1. Review the first two books of the trilogy by identifying the genre, narrator, protagonist(s), antagonist(s), the inciting incident, and the reversal for Acts One and Two.

2. Based on the information that you identified in question 1, describe your expectations for *Mockingjay*. Include your thoughts about questions that Collins needs to answer in order for the ending to be, in your estimation, satisfactory.

3. Think about the title *Mockingjay*. Based on the title and your prior knowledge of the series, what do you expect to happen in this book?

4. What can you tell about the *Mockingjay* from the part titles:

   Part I: "The Ashes"; Part II: "The Assault"; Part III: "The Assassin"?

   How do they seem to relate to the book title? How do they seem to relate to the titles of the three parts of *The Hunger Games*—

   Part I: "The Tributes"; Part II: "The Games"; Part III "The Victor"?

   How do they relate to the part titles of *Catching Fire*—

   Part I: "The Spark"; Part II: "The Quell"; Part III: "The Enemy"?

5. Read the first five paragraphs. Identify each reference, attitude, etc. that you understand more deeply because you've already read *The Hunger Games* and *Catching Fire*.

6. Given everything you know at this point, what do you predict will be the main plot developments in Act Three of this trilogy? What do you think the confrontations will involve? What do you predict will be the climax of the series?

Chapter 1

Vocabulary

point of reference 3 something used as a starting point for understanding

orient myself 3 recognize my position in relation to my surroundings

incineration 3 being burnt to ashes

refugees 3 someone forced to leave home by war or disaster

concussion 4 temporary unconsciousness from a blow to the head

weaning ... off 5 getting her used to relying less and less on

incinerated 5 destroyed by burning

decomposition 5 state of decay or rotting

carrion 5 decaying flesh of dead animals

scavengers 5 animals that live on carrion

firestorm 6 destructive fire caused by bombing

retribution 6 punishment that is considered to be just and deserved

chaos 6 total disorder and confusion

belch 6 burp loudly

absolve 6 set free from blame or guilt

wherewithal 6 means needed for a particular purpose

resistance 6 refusal to accept or comply

oppression 6 prolonged government injustice

perilous 6 full of risk or danger

lash 7 blow of a whip

loath 7 reluctant

stragglers 7 those lagging behind

glean 7 collect bit by bit

compartments 8 separate sections or small rooms

pox 8 viral disease causing a rash

infertile 8 not capable of parenting children

breeding stock 8 animals valued for their genetic material

genetic diversity 8 variety of genes

implantation 8 placing an embryo into a mother's womb

embryos 8 unborn, still developing mammals

refuse 9 garbage

rubble 9 debris from destroyed buildings

lacerated 9 cut or torn very deeply

wreckage 9 remains of something destroyed

mishmash 10 confused mixture

flaw 10 fault or imperfection

split end 10 division at the tip of a hair

rallying point 10 something that everyone can support

mouthpiece 11 person or organization who speaks for another

firebrand 11 passionate person w/ radical views

conscious 11 no longer unconscious; awake and aware

irreversible 12 not able to be undone

interrogation 12 harsh questioning of a suspected or known criminal or enemy

enigmatic 12 difficult to interpret

outweigh 13 be more significant than

extend 13 reach out

redeeming quality 13 attribute that makes up for other, less desirable, characteristics

unceremoniously 13 w/out civilities; lacking courtesy

inexplicably 14 w/out being able to be understood

bugs 14 hidden microphones

noteworthy 14 important

infuriates 15 makes extremely angry and irritable

drug-induced 15 caused by drugs

Journal and Discussion Topics

1. Now that you've read the first chapter, what do you think Part I of *Mockingjay* will be about? What evidence supports your conclusions?

2. What parallels do you find between the opening of *Mockingjay* and the openings of *HG* and *CF*? What differences?

3. In this chapter, Katniss mentions several reasons for having returning to 12. Identify them.

4. What contrast does Katniss draw between Gale and herself?

5. Is Katniss's current opinion of herself grounded in fact and rational? Explain your answer.

6. What is Katniss trying to demonstrate to others in this chapter? Why is this a matter of concern?

7. In *third-person limited point of view*, the main character—the one from whose perspective the story is told by the narrator—is often named and described to some degree in a paragraph or several close to the beginning of the book. In a series, this information is already known, but it is often repeated in every book in case readers have forgotten since reading the previous volume.

But this approach would be awkward in a series with *first-person narration*. Explain how the first-person narrator reiterates basic facts about herself and other important characters in Chapter 1 of *Mockingjay*, referring to *foreshadowing*, *flashback*, and *recap*, as appropriate. What information that is covered at the beginning of *HG* and *CF* is omitted here? Why do you think that is?

8. Which new characters are introduced in Chapter 1? How full are the descriptions of them? What does this suggest to you about their importance?

9. How does a knowledge of the interactions between Katniss and Buttercup in *HG* (pp. 3–4) and *CF* (p. 7) inform your understanding of Katniss's interactions with Buttercup in the first chapter of *Mockingjay*? What other influences are at work?

10. How does Katniss make the connection between the rose and President Snow? Why does she call its smell "artificial"?

11. Reread the end of *CF*, beginning with the paragraph that starts, "Until one time, I open my eyes and find someone I cannot block . . ." Consider what expectations it raises for the beginning of *Mockingjay*. So far, have these expectations been fulfilled or subverted? Explain your answer. Then tell how a reader's experience would be different without this expectation.

12. Present an argument for what you believe is the inciting incident for the plot of *Mockingjay*, as you currently understand it. Support your position with information and quotations as appropriate.

13. What expectations does Chapter 1 create for you about the plot of *Mockingjay*?

14. Speculate on what has happened to Peeta and the other tributes that were not rescued by Plutarch et al.

15. Katniss recalls (*MJ*, p. 6) Snow's statement about Katniss providing a spark that "may grow to an inferno that destroys Panem" (repeated from *CF* p. 23). She then presents her analysis of that conversation: "It turns out he wasn't exaggerating or simply trying to scare me. He was, perhaps, genuinely attempting to enlist my help." Consider the evidence for Katniss's conclusions. Citing evidence in *CF*, analyze Katniss's analysis. Then state your understanding of Collins having Katniss say this: what narrative purpose(s) do you think it is intended to serve? Is it successful, in your opinion?

16. Summarize the chapter from Plutarch's point of view. Be sure to tell only what he knows or could reasonably be expected to know.

Summary

Katniss Everdeen, the first-person narrator, stands in the ruins of the house in which she grew up in District 12. It is a month after the Capitol firebombed everything except the Victor's Village. She has been allowed to return by the powers that be in District 13 in the hopes that she will become the Mockingjay—the symbol of the revolution which President Coin of 13 and Plutarch Heavensbee, former Head Gamemaker, are leading. Katniss is still suffering both from the concussion she received at the end of *CF* and from Post-Traumatic Stress Disorder (PTSD hereafter). Gale, who is in the hovercraft that brought her to 12 from 13, offers to join her on the ground, but Katniss wants to be alone.

Walking through the ruins and among the corpses of her neighbors, she recalls President's Snows words to her when he visited her house, and she believes them true and herself responsible for the destruction around her, while Gale—along with Mrs. Everdeen and Prim—is responsible for having saved the 800 or so District 12 survivors, who were welcomed into District 13. Katniss has since learned that the welcome was not rooted in kindness—District 13 has suffered an epidemic and needs to increase its population.

After visiting the Mellark's bakery, of which nothing is left but the melted oven, and remarking that none of Peeta's family escaped alive, Katniss trips over the remains of the gallows in the town square and heads for the Victor's Village, asking herself why she returned to 12, wondering what she is going to do with regard to being the Mockingjay as she enters her house and picks up her parents' wedding photo, the family book, and one of Prim's hair ribbons to take with her. Greeted by a hiss in the kitchen, she finds that Buttercup has survived and, coaxing him over by mentioning Prim, stuffs him in a game bag to take back to 13 with her. She goes upstairs to her room to collect her father's hunting jacket, but inexplicably, her palms start sweating. Searching around, she finds a perfect white rose, clearly left for her by President Snow, letting her know that he can still find her and that she and those she loves are far from safe.

Chapter 2

Peeta's 1st Interview

Vocabulary

recovery 16 return to a normal state
loathsome 16 causing hatred or disgust
substantial 17 large; sizable
refuge 17 place of safety
last resort 17 place to go for safety when nowhere else is left
humanity 17 all human beings
strenuous 17 requiring great exertion
vigilance 17 careful watchfulness
tattoos 18 permanent or temporary ink images on the skin
indelible 18 unable to be removed
resistant 18 unaffected by
breaks down 18 dissolves
forgo 18 go without
imprinted 18 stamped with a schedule
get with the program 18 behave as is expected
air duct 18 tube for the passage of air through a building
frugal 18 living simply and plainly w/out much expense
criminal activity 18 actions that are illegal
very portrait 18 personification (used sarcastically)
excess 18 using more than necessary
clockwork precision 18 detailed exactness
mentally disoriented 19 confused
ramblings 19 confused, unfocused speeches
reflection 19 serious thought
downtime 19 unscheduled time for relaxing
gauge 19 estimate
adoration 19 feeling of deep love and respect
status 20 position that gives certain rights, privileges, and possibly responsibilities
high-tech 20 employing the latest and most sophisticated electronics
computerized 20 converted to a being operated or controlled by computer
replaying 20 playing back footage already seen
eternal 20 everlasting
deprived of ... 21 experiencing a damaging lack of ...

reconcile 21 bring back into friendly relations
upholstered 21 padded and covered w/ material to add comfort (of furniture)
pawns 21 people used by others for their own purposes
conciliatory 24 intended to make peace
distraught 24 deeply upset
consumption 25 drinking
home-brewed 25 alcoholic drink or beer made at home
transition 25 change
seclusion 25 state of being private or in solitude
deemed fit 25 considered well and healthy
cast ... off 25 ended a relationship with ...
wryly 25 w/ dry or mocking humor
cease-fire 26 temporary stop of fighting
solar batteries 26 batteries powered by the sun
absorption 26 process of being absorbed
collaborating 26 working together
undeniable 26 obvious; unquestionable
complicity 26 working together in illegal activities
outrage 27 extreme anger or indignation
jerk 27 MM pull sharply
right-hand 27 most important
lackey 27 derogatory word for someon who serves w/ excessive obedience
jerk 28 MM obnoxious or contemptible person
demotion 28 reduction in rank or status
nukes 28 nuclear weapons
nuclear war 28 war fought using nuclear weapons
decimated 29 killed a large percentage of the population
gene pool 29 available variety of genes in a population that interbreeds
breeders 29 those who have offspring
militaristic 29 following an aggressive military policy
rebel base 29 core group of rebels
imprisoned 30 locked up; jailed
corpse-littered 30 covered w/ dead bodies
alignment 31 lining up evenly
concise 31 to the point; w/out unnecessary movement

Journal and Discussion Topics

1. In this chapter, Katniss offers a third explanation of why she went back to District 12. What do you make of her comment to Gale about this?

2. Think of another story in which order and sameness are key elements of a culture. Compare Collins's use of sameness in District 13 with your understanding of how it is used in the other story. What does it represent or mean in each case?

3. Earlier in the trilogy, Collins used the strawman technique to set up false expectations in order to increase the reader's surprise at developments. How does she use that technique in this chapter

4. What has happened to Haymitch since *CF*?

5. Compare and contrast Katniss's attempts to give first-aid to Gale in this chapter to her experiences caring for Peeta.

6. What changes in Katniss's view of District 13 in this chapter?

7. Do you agree with Gale about Peeta's motivation? Explain your answer.

8. What does the contrast in Katniss's and Gale's handling of the pencils convey to you?

9. What reasons does Peeta offer in defense of a cease-fire? How does Katniss counter them? What is her response to his rhetoric?

10. Identify any instances of foreshadowing, recap, or flashback in this chapter

11 Summarize the chapter from Gale's point of view.

Summary

Back in the hovercraft, Katniss and Gale reconnect over their grief for their lost home. As they reach 13, Katniss chronicles the true history of 13: they had made a deal with the Capitol and moved their operations almost entirely underground. She then remarks on the current, highly structured lifestyle and her disregard for it, excused till now by her classification as being "mentally disoriented." Landing in 13, Katniss goes to the room assigned to her family and delivers Buttercup and the other treasures she saved.

As they head to dinner, Gale's communicuff beeps with a message calling him and Katniss to Command. Contrary to her expectations, this is not an intense Mockingjay recruitment session but a gathering to watch a Capitol broadcast that Katniss cannot imagine as being interesting, until she sees that Caesar Flickerman is interviewing a healthy-looking Peeta. The fact that he is alive and apparently hasn't been tortured is more than she had dared hope. He gives an insightful report on what's it's like to be in the arena and a recap of the plot points at the end of *CF*. He defends Katniss's innocence and lack of knowledge of what she was doing when she blew the force field. In conclusion, he calls for a cease-fire, revealing that he is complicit with the Capitol. Hearing the others in Command condemn Peeta as a traitor, Katniss flees with Gale's assistance, despite not having been dismissed by President Coin. He catches up with her at her hiding place in the supply closet, where she avoids people and work assignments. Gale's analysis helps Katniss see that the Games haven't stopped: Peeta is still trying to keep her alive. But she can't accept the idea of a cease-fire, and defends Peeta. Gale comments that he would have no reservations about killing everyone working for the Capitol if he could, and asks what Katniss is going to do. Peeta's "ploy" has given her clarity, and now she is determined to be the Mockingjay.

Strategy 2

Directions:
First, read the information. Then, answer the question or questions.

A **continuity error** is an unintentional inconsistency that can be more or less important. A change of eye color, for example, is unlikely to faze, and may not even be noticed by, many readers. But other unexplained inconsistencies may make it difficult for readers to interpret the story or to trust the writer.

But the world *is* inconsistent, you might respond. Yes, the world is inconsistent. People can be inconsistent in their actions, preferences, and attitudes. But fiction is not real life, and in order for readers to understand stories and their characters, we hold them to a higher standard of consistency than is found in life, unless either the story is about inconsistency or the lack of continuity is explained in some understandable way.

Some people go on a hunt for movie or book continuity errors as a game. Since movies are assembled from many, many separate takes, lapses are likely, and there's a certain sense of being a really attentive viewer that comes with spotting a mistake. But if you're looking for mistakes, you're not engaged in the story. There is no suggestion here that you treat stories like this. But as you engage in imagining stories, thinking critically about texts, and analyzing narratives, it is possible that you will imagine scenes, ask questions, or consider possibilities that will reveal continuity errors to you.

Here's an example of how an apparent continuity error might unfold: On page 20, Gale reports to Katniss that they're needed in Command. Suppose you asked a simple question: Why? Katniss assumes that it will be a continuation of "relentless Mockingjay" recruitment. Given that neither Plutarch nor Coin has seen her since the trip to District 12—a trip that was allowed because Katniss made it a condition of becoming the Mockingjay (p. 3)—it's logical that they would want to debrief her and see if she's convinced. But that's not it. They request her presence in Command to see whatever-the-Capitol-is-about-to-show. There is no evidence that they have an insider in the Capitol broadcast studio, so presumably the most they know when sending the message is that Caesar Flickerman will interview Peeta. That the camera pulls back *after* Katniss arrives and the manner of Caesar's greeting to Peeta suggest that this is the beginning of the broadcast. Does it seem to you that it was a smart move for Plutarch and Coin to make? Does it seem to you like a gamble they would take, without knowing if seeing the destruction of District 12 had already convinced Katniss to buy in? Given their intelligence and strategic outlooks, do you think they would throw caution to the winds, and allow Katniss to see something they hadn't previewed? Collins does not explore this, but we can.

Katniss planned to kill Peeta to prevent his being tortured by the Capitol (*CF*, p. 383) and still believes that Peeta would be better off dead (*MJ*, p. 4). Watching the broadcast live seems to be a very dangerous move, since any sign that Peeta had been tortured could completely unbalance Katniss, destroying her ability to be the Mockingjay. Even if he were in perfect health, seeing him is sure to distract her. Would they take such a risk? It seems unlikely. The choice left to the reader is to reevaluate Plutarch and Coin as desperate and/or cavalier or to identify a continuity error. Since we expect internal consistency in characterization, this is likely to be a continuity error and is far more serious than a change of eye color.

1. Look for other inconsistencies as you continue to read.

Chapter 3 Mockingjay with Conditions

Vocabulary

recuperating 32 recovering from physical or mental ill health

confiscated 32 took away; removed

immunity 34 protection from any penalties or punishments

reneging on 34 going back on

validity 34 state of being legally binding

death warrant 34 official order for execution

nutrition 35 science of providing appropriate food for each person's needs

hoarding 36 hiding food for future use

unimpressed 38 not moved to a favorable opinion by the evidence

nonissue 38 a given

deducted 39 taken away

tracker anklets 39 electronic device that encircles the ankle and monitors location

malice 39 ill will

defection 39 change of loyalties

dispose of 40 turn my affections from (used metaphorically)

pardoned 40 forgiven

tribunal 41 court of justice

resonant 41 deep and ringing

tallying 41 calculating; figuring out

ultimatum 41 condition or requirement necessary for continued negotiations

national security 41 related to the safety and survival of the state

assembly 41 meeting

rickety 41 poorly drawn

sole 42 only

adhere to 42 stick to; follow

unthinkable 42 out of the question

gruel 42 thin cereal of cooked grain

side action 42 something done off the record

incorruptible 42 having integrity; unable to be bribed

bound 42 MM placed in a cover for protection

utilitarian 43 made for function alone

reinforcements 43 strong, protective structures

holding out on 43 refusing to share real opinion and feelings

airtime 44 time during which a show is broadcast

assault 44 attack (used metaphorically)

spots 44 short video segments

well intended 45 meant to be kind

claustrophobia 45 fear of small, closed-in spaces

caustic 45 acidic; sharp; bitter

antiseptic 45 cleaner that kills and/or prevents the growth of bacteria

double-checks 46 looks back at again to be sure

discrepancies 46 unexplained changes from the agreed upon plan

cowed 46 terrorized into submission

Journal and Discussion Questions

1. From what you know, evaluate Katniss's chances of successfully acting in propos.

2. Do you think Katniss's conclusions about Cinna are valid? Explain.

3. What did you think Plutarch's surprise was going to be at first?

4. How does this chapter highlight differences between life in 12 and 13?

5. Given what you know of 13, why do you imagine the prep team was imprisoned?

6. Use the Choice Analysis Tool (pp. 42–3) to analyze Katniss's decision to be the Mockingjay.

7. Summarize the chapter from Prim's point of view.

Summary

Unable to sleep, Katniss sits holding the pearl from Peeta. Prim awakens and over Katniss's protests, wraps her in a blanket. Katniss tells Prim that she's going to agree to be the Mockingjay but is worried about Peeta. Prim says Katniss is in a position to ask for what she wants, and she decides to ask for immunity for Peeta. At breakfast with Gale, she gets the idea of asking to be able to hunt, and as they head to Command to make her announcement, he suggests she add Buttercup to the list. In command, she makes these demands, plus immunity for all the captured tributes, having the immunity commitment announced in public, and that she be allowed to kill Snow. All are granted but the last, which Coin says she'll flip Katniss for when the time comes. Only now does Plutarch show Katniss Cinna's sketchbook of outfits for Katniss as Mockingjay and reveal that Beetee has crafted her a special weapon. Her first task is to appear in propos, to be broadcast across Panem using Beetee's expertise. He announces a surprise for Katniss, and leads her deep into 13, where they are shocked to find her prep team imprisoned.

Chapter 4

Vocabulary

vises 47 tools that grip an object firmly so it cannot shift while work is being done on it

infractions 48 instances of rule-breaking

density 48 inability to understand

composure 49 feeling of calm and control

misery 49 excrement, urine, and possibly vomit (used as a euphemism)

consternation 49 feeling of intense dismay and surprise

verdict 50 decision

flogging 50 whipping

pedigree 50 ancestry

liability 50 cause of increased risk

masterminded 50 did all the complex planning for

beauticians 50 experts in hair styling, manicures, etc.

icily 50 in a hostile manner

disposable 51 able to be easily forgotten or gotten rid of

instability 51 lack of stability or steadiness

on edge 51 nervous

immersion 51 opportunity to be completely surrounded by

overrides 51 takes precedence over

handheld communicator 52 walkie-talkie

revoked 52 taken away

abide 52 put up w/; be able to tolerate

bask in 52 make the most of; lie back to fully expose oneself to

broken in 52 worn to the point of becoming comfortable for the owner

scorching 53 burning hot

strung up 54 hung

palatable 55 tasty

bound 55 MM likely

mobile 56 able to walk

unraveling 56 untying

therapy 56 treatment

nudge 56 gentle poke with the elbow to get someone's attention

construed 56 understood; interpreted

traitorous 56 betraying Panem; disloyal

frail 57 weak and vulnerable

frailty 57 state of being weak and vulnerable

consented 57 agreed

deviance 58 wavering; departure

terminated 58 ended

step out of line 58 break the rules; disobey

Journal and Discussion Questions

1. What conclusions did reading about the prep team's punishment lead you to?

2. Do you think Katniss is justified in being concerned about Coin? Do you think Plutarch is justified in his unconcern? Explain.

3. Given Katniss's past reflections on her shoes, what do you make of her comments in this chapter?

4. How is hunting in 13 different from hunting in 12?

5. Explain the crux of Gale's and Katniss's disagreement in your own words.

6. Based on the evidence in *Mockingjay*, write a character study of Gale. Based on your analysis of his traits and attitudes, what role do you think he will play in the remainder of the book?

7 Summarize the chapter from Mrs. Everdeen's point of view.

Summary

After learning that the prep team is being punished for stealing bread, Plutarch has them released on his authority, and Katniss takes them to her mother in 13's hospital. While waiting for Mrs. Everdeen's assessment—which turns out to be that there is no permanent damage—Katniss speculates aloud on the consequences of getting on Coin's bad side, though Plutarch is unconcerned.

Gale and Katniss go hunting, and as they fall into familiar routines, Katniss is "as close to happiness" as she can be in the current situation. But then Gale asks why Katniss cares about her prep team, and the differences in their views are far-reaching, and they return to 13 without resolving them.

As the population gathers for Coin's assembly, Katniss notices Finnick among the patients her mother brings, and in speaking to him, realizes that she forgot to ask for immunity for Annie Cresta. She goes up to Coin and adds Annie to her list, and returns to Finnick's side. Coin announces the conditions and gives the population of 13 time to respond among themselves, and many are put off by the plan to forgive those they see as possible enemies. She concludes by saying something she did not say to Katniss: that any failure on Katniss's part to fulfill her mission as Mockingjay—in either "motive or deed"—will annul the agreement, and the fate of the imprisoned victors and Katniss would be determined by the laws of District 13.

Chapter 5

Prepped for Propos; New Bows; Propo Flop

Vocabulary

power player 59 one who employs tactics to increase her own power and influence
ensnaring 59 trapping
groom 59 prepare for presentation
brand 59 label
enhancements 60 changes to make her look "better" than she does naturally
gaudy 60 showy and in bad taste
knickknacks 60 small objects that have little or no value
gag reflex 61 involuntary reaction to prevent choking, often in response to disgusting smells or sights
sullenly 62 showing one's bad temper
dismissive 62 unconcerned; showing that one considers something unimportant
inwardly 62 inside, w/out outward expression
covert 62 secret; meant to be concealed
imprisonment 63 being locked up
consistency 63 texture; thickness
caving in 64 giving way; yielding
replication 65 later version of an original
hover 65 holding position in the air
convalescence 65 recovery from injury or illness
alight 65 bright
aerodynamics 65 the way air flows around objects in motion
vulnerabilities 66 weaknesses
meltdown 67 mental collapse; loss of mental balance
weaponry 67 types of weapons
retinal 67 of the retina (the layer at the back of the eyeball)

DNA 67 the material that carries genetic information (deoxyribonucleic acid)
scans 67 processes of examining a body part w/ a device for comparison to a database to verify ID and access privileges
metal detectors 67 metal locators
bizarre 67 ridiculous
influx 67 arrival of many people
immigrants 67 people who move to a foreign land
armored 67 covered w/ a metal layer to defend against attack
self-evident 68 obvious
scopes 68 view finders
gadgetry 68 high-end devices that add functionality
hefts 68 lifts something heavy
fashion accessory 69 item created to enhance the wearer's outfit
incendiary 70 designed to set objects on fire
shaft 70 body of an arrow - the straight stick
deactivate 70 stop the functioning of
don 70 dress in; put on
soundstage 70 studio setup w/ properties desirable for recording sound
via 70 by way of
intercom 70 device providing two-way communication
booth 70 control room for film production
monitor 70 television receiver used to test footage before broadcast
acerbic 72 sharp; sarcastic; cutting

Journal and Discussion Questions

1. What is the narrrative purpose of the recap at the beginning of this chapter?

2. Katniss finds her prep ironic for several reasons. Explain.

3. What do you gather from Katniss's comparison of "Capitol Octavia" and "District 13 Octavia"?

4. Katniss has to tug up her sleeve to see her schedule (p. 51), and sleeve length comes up again on p. 61. Based on story evidence, why would the efficient, precise District 13 residents design uniforms that don't keep the schedule in view?

5. Kataniss "sighs inwardly" at the idea of taking her preps to lunch. What basis in anything that has come before do you find for this attitude?

6. Thinking about narrative function, explain why Collins includes the second argument between Katniss and Gale as a flashback at lunch rather than in time order?

7. What do you think Katniss finds disconcerting about Gale's and Beetee's conversation?

8. Analyze the meanings of the bandage Katniss is fitted with for the propo.

9. Why does Finnick say people will want to kill, kiss, or be Katniss?

10. What do the silence and Haymitch's comment convey about Katniss's performance?

11. Summarize the chapter from Beetee's point of view.

Summary

As Katniss soaks in a tub of bubbles, she identifies Coin as a power player, the latest person to be using her, with Coin being the first publically to say that Katniss poses a potential threat. Getting out of the tub, Katniss contrasts the Capitol and District 13 versions of her prep team. The preps bring Katniss to "Beauty Base Zero," but don't know what to do with the scar on her forearm where Johanna dug the tracker out. They break, and Katniss takes the preps to lunch. Posy Hawthorne's admiration of Octavia helps ease awkwardness, and Gale attempts to keep conversation going in what Katniss recognizes as a peace offering. She reveals that she and Gale had had a second argument the previous day about whether Coin's surprise "countercondition" was justified, leaving Katniss questioning if Gale is on her side or Coin's.

After lunch, as Gale and Katniss head for Special Defense, they briefly revisit the argument, with Katniss recognizing that she appreciates Gale's honesty. They are led to Beetee, who works from a wheelchair, and the conversation between Beetee and Gale about killing hummingbirds disconcerts Katniss. As they head for the weapons room, Beetee gives Katniss a message for Finnick about a new trident he's designed for him. Katniss is surprised by the security checks at the armory and wonders if they were implemented due to the refugees from District 12. The armory holds row upon row of weapons, including military bows, one of which Gale chooses upon Beetee's offer. With Beetee out of the room, they discuss killing people vs. animals for food, and Katniss doesn't know how to explain the consequences of killing a person to Gale, so says nothing. Beetee returns with the bow he's made for Katniss, ignoring (he says) the request to make a bow for show and building it as a weapon that takes regular, incendiary, and explosive arrows and responds to Katniss's voice to turn on and shut down. Armed with her bow, she returns to prep for the propo. Katniss is impressed by her appearance on the monitor. She is given a line to say in the aftermath of a pretend battle the Fulvia describes. But after Katniss speaks the line, everybody is silent, and Haymitch breaks in on the intercom, to deride her ineffective performance.

Strategy 3

Understanding the Meaning of Silence

Directions:
First, read the information. Then, answer the question or questions.

In real life as well as fiction, silence can be positive, negative, or neutral and signal respect, surprise, digust, concealment, disagreement, calm, sleep, etc. Collins has 10 uses of *silent, silence,* or *silently* in Chapters 1–5 in *Mockingjay,* and it's worth examining how she uses it and how we can interpret it. These two groups of questions can help you determine the meaaning of silence in any particular instance:

Immediate Context

- Who or what is being silent? (Is it a person or animal? the environment? a machine?)

- What are the usual meanings of silence for whatever is being silent? (Silence for a machine often indicates that it's broken or that it is well crafted; silence for a toddler often means sleep or getting into mischief.)

Broader Context

- What's the situation? (What's the time of day, season? Where is the scene set?)

- Was the silence expected? (When a baby is put down for a nap, silence is expected eventually, possibly after a period of fussing.)

- Does the silence contrast with something immediately preceding or following? (At a performance, there is usually a moment of silence before the performance starts and after it ends.)

Use the questions above to analyze the 10 uses of silence so far in *Mockingjay*:

1. p. 7 "and the Seam became so silent, people could hear one another's heartbeats."

2. p. 16 "We sit in silence for the rest of the trip to 13. . . ."

3. p. 22 "In the silence that follows. . . ."

4. p. 37 ". . . everyone waits in silence while I sit at the table and scrawl out my list."

5. p. 37 "I shut my eyes and start to recite silently, *My name is Katniss Everdeen. . . .*"

6. p. 40 "'. . . Peeta will be pardoned.' Dead silence."; p. 45 "A door swings silently shut. . . ."

7. p. 51 "We wait in silence until my mother finds us."

8. p. 53 "Silent, needing no words to communicate . . ."

9. p. 69 "The top opens on silent hinges."

10. p. 72 "There's dead silence on the set."

Vocabulary

limitations 73 restrictions; failings

disjointed 74 unconnected; not unified

does someone's bidding 75 follows someone's orders

inhumanity 75 brutal and cruel treatment

unscripted 75 not planned in advance with memorized lines, but spontaneous

controversial 76 unlikely to be universally accepted

spontaneity 76 acting on impulse, rather than based on a script

illuminated 76 backlit; shown on a display like a computer monitor

adjourns 77 ends

ventilation 77 system to provide fresh air to the facility

heart of hearts 77 deepest being

optimism 78 confidence

earpiece 78 microphone that fits in the ear

sidelong 80 sideways (so as not to be noticed)

close-cropped 80 short

laterally 80 to the side

involuntarily 80 w/out intending to

defenseless 81 unable to defend themselves

counterattack 81 military response to an attack

snugness 81 close fit

witty 82 clever

comeback 82 answer; retort

recruiting 83 enlisting; persuading (someone) to sign up for

deprivation 83 lacking basic necessities, like enough food

mind-set 83 way of looking at the world

bloodlust 83 desire to kill

supply chain 83 source of goods and products

republic 83 form of elected representative government

centralized government 84 central authority to which smaller political units give power for effective management

Journal and Discussion Questions

1. Why might readers who recall the earlier books well react differently to the end of Chapter 5 and the beginning of Chapter 6 than readers who don't? Explain.

2. Based on Katniss's response to Haymitch's reminder that he is her mentor, what do you predict will happen?

3. How do Plutarch's plans for a new government affect your conception of him?

4. What do you conclude about Cinna from information revealed in *Mockingjay*?

5. Summarize the chapter from Boggs's point of view.

Summary

Although Katniss acknowledges that Haymitch is correct, his comment and the knowledge that he has a role in the proceedings leads her to walk out on the session. Seeing that a different approach is needed, Haymitch calls a meeting the following day and succeeds in demonstrating that Katniss does the best when she is spontaneous and unscripted; hence real combat situations are the settings most likely to evoke the emotion and passion the rebels need the Mockingjay to display. In response to Coin's question about her possible death, Katniss tells her to make sure to get footage. Dalton adds that they should get rid of the face-obscuring makeup.

As the meeting adjourns, Haymitch asks to speak to Katniss privately, and they finally confront each other over each of their failures in keeping Peeta safe. Haymitch concludes by reminding Katniss that he's her mentor, and that since he's going along in the hovercraft for the "almost combat" shoot, she should listen to him. Katniss only says, "We'll see."

Dressed in the armor Cinna designed, with a gas mask, an earpiece, and her three types of arrows in a sheath on her back, Katniss is heading out when Finnick, still recovering, appears in a hospital gown, wanting to go. Thinking quickly, Katniss redirects him to Beetee to pick up his knew trident, avoiding a scene and leading to her first significant interaction with Boggs, Coin's right-hand man.

In the hangar, they discuss the choice both sides has made—so far—to use only conventional, not nuclear weapons. Katniss enters the hovercraft and is greeted by Fulvia, who bemoans the loss of the makeup. Realizing that she has no idea what's going on in the war, Katniss gets an explanation from Plutarch, which includes the favored status of District 2. Gale asks who would run the government if the rebels win, and Plutarch says they plan to form a republic with representatives, as had once been the case. He hands out suicide pills, and Katniss discovers Cinna's outfit has a special pocket for it: he has, she thinks, thought of everything.

Strategy 4   Justifying a Revolution

There have been, and are, many revolutions, and those who revolt sometimes offer an attempt to justify their intent to overthrow an existing government. Such was the case with the American Revolution, as documented in the Declaration of Independence.

1. Make a list of the complaints in the United States Declaration of Independence that also apply to the citizens of Panem, supporting your choices with examples from the trilogy. Then discuss whether, in your opinion, revolution in Panem is justified.

2. The Declaration of Independence emphasizes the attempts the colonists have made to work with the existing government. Explain why there is no parallel in Panem.

3. Why do you think Plutarch Heavensbee and President Coin feel no need to pen a declaration of independence for the districts of Panem?

The Unanimous Declaration of the Thirteen United States of America

In Congress, July 4, 1776

When in the Course of human events, it becomes necessary for one people to dissolve the political bands which have connected them with another, and to assume among the powers of the earth, the separate and equal station to which the Laws of Nature and of Nature's God entitle them, a decent respect to the opinions of mankind requires that they should declare the causes which impel them to the separation.

We hold these truths to be self-evident, that all men are created equal; that they are endowed by their Creator with certain unalienable rights; that among these are Life, Liberty, and the pursuit of Happiness; that, to secure these rights, governments are instituted among Men, deriving their just powers from the consent of the governed; that whenever any form of government becomes destructive of these ends, it is the right of the people to alter or to abolish it, and to institute new government, laying its foundation on such principles, and organizing its powers in such form, as to them shall seem most likely to effect their safety and happiness. Prudence, indeed, will dictate that governments long established should not be changed for light and transient causes; and accordingly all experience hath shown that mankind are more disposed to suffer, while evils are sufferable than to right themselves by abolishing the forms to which they are accustomed. But when a long train of abuses and usurpations, pursuing invariably the same object, evinces a design to reduce them under absolute despotism, it is their right, it is their duty, to throw off such government, and to provide new guards for their future security. Such has been the patient sufferance of these colonies; and such is now the necessity which constrains them to alter their former systems of government. The history of the present King of Great Britain is a history of repeated injuries and usurpations, all having in direct object the establishment of an absolute tyranny over these states. To prove this, let facts be submitted to a candid world.

He has refused his assent to laws, the most wholesome and necessary for the public good.

He has forbidden his governors to pass laws of immediate and pressing importance, unless suspended in their operation till his assent should be obtained; and, when so suspended, he has utterly neglected to attend to them.

He has refused to pass other laws for the accommodation of large districts of people, unless those people would relinquish the right of representation in the legislature, a right inestimable to them, and formidable to tyrants only.

He has called together legislative bodies at places unusual uncomfortable, and distant from the depository of their public records, for the sole purpose of fatiguing them into compliance with his measures.

He has dissolved representative houses repeatedly, for opposing, with manly firmness, his invasions on the rights of the people.

He has refused for a long time, after such dissolutions, to cause others to be elected; whereby the legislative powers, incapable of annihilation, have returned to the people at large for their exercise; the state remaining, in the mean time, exposed to all the dangers of invasions from without and convulsions within.

He has endeavored to prevent the population of these states; for that purpose obstructing the laws for naturalization of foreigners; refusing to pass others to encourage their migration hither, and raising the conditions of new appropriations of lands.

He has obstructed the administration of justice, by refusing his assent to laws for establishing judiciary powers.

He has made judges dependent on his will alone, for the tenure of their offices, and the amount and payment of their salaries.

He has erected a multitude of new offices, and sent hither swarms of officers to harass our people and eat out their substance.

He has kept among us, in times of peace, standing armies, without the consent of our legislatures.

He has affected to render the military independent of, and superior to, the civil power.

He has combined with others to subject us to a jurisdiction foreign to our Constitution and unacknowledged by our laws, giving his assent to their acts of pretended legislation:

For quartering large bodies of armed troops among us;

For protecting them, by a mock trial, from punishment for any murders which they should commit on the inhabitants of these states;

For cutting off our trade with all parts of the world;

For imposing taxes on us without our consent;

For depriving us, in many cases, of the benefits of trial by jury;

For transporting us beyond seas, to be tried for pretended offenses;

For abolishing the free system of English laws in a neighboring province, establishing therein an arbitrary government, and enlarging its boundaries, so as to render it at once an example and fit instrument for introducing the same absolute rule into these colonies;

For taking away our charters, abolishing our most valuable laws, and altering fundamentally the forms of our governments;

For suspending our own legislatures, and declaring themselves invested with power to legislate for us in all cases whatsoever.

He has abdicated government here, by declaring us out of his protection and waging war against us.

He has plundered our seas, ravaged our coasts, burned our towns, and destroyed the lives of our people.

He is at this time transporting large armies of foreign mercenaries to complete the works of death, desolation, and tyranny already begun with circumstances of cruelty and perfidy scarcely paralleled in the most barbarous ages, and totally unworthy the head of a civilized nation.

He has constrained our fellow-citizens, taken captive on the high seas, to bear arms against their country, to become the executioners of their friends and brethren, or to fall themselves by their hands.

He has excited domestic insurrection among us, and has endeavored to bring on the inhabitants of our frontiers the merciless Indian savages, whose known rule of warfare is an undistinguished destruction of all ages, sexes, and conditions.

In every stage of these oppressions we have petitioned for redress in the most humble terms; our repeated petitions have been answered only by repeated injury. A prince, whose character is thus marked by every act which may define a tyrant, is unfit to be the ruler of a free people.

Nor have we been wanting in our attentions to our British brethren. We have warned them, from time to time, of attempts by their legislature to extend an unwarrantable jurisdiction over us. We have reminded them of the circumstances of our emigration and settlement here. We have appealed to their native justice and magnanimity; and we have conjured them, by the ties of our common kindred, to disavow these usurpations which would inevitably interrupt our connections and correspondence. They too, have been deaf to the voice of justice and of consanguinity. We must, therefore, acquiesce in the necessity which denounces our separation, and hold them as we hold the rest of mankind, enemies in war, in peace friends.

WE, THEREFORE, the REPRESENTATIVES of the UNITED STATES OF AMERICA, in General Congress assembled, appealing to the Supreme Judge of the world for the rectitude of our intentions, do, in the name and by the authority of the good people of these colonies solemnly publish and declare, That these United Colonies are, and of right ought to be, FREE AND INDEPENDENT STATES; that they are absolved from all allegiance to the British crown and that all political connection between them and the state of Great Britain is, and ought to be, totally dissolved; and that, as free and independent states, they have full power to levy war, conclude peace, contract alliances, establish commerce, and do all other acts and things which independent states may of right do. And for the support of this declaration, with a firm reliance on the protection of Divine Providence, we mutually pledge to each other our Lives, our Fortunes, and our sacred Honor.

Chapter 7

The Hospital in District 8; Combat

Vocabulary

asphalt 85 mixture of pitch w/ sand or gravel for paving roads

disembarks 85 gets off an aircraft

retracts 85 pulls back

burly 85 large and strong

medics 85 military healthcare workers who provide first aid in battle

confronted 86 brought face-to-face w/

double take 86 delayed reaction

comply 86 do what they're told

spanking-new 87 both new and striking

accusation 87 suggestion of wrongdoing

contagious disease 87 disease that is transmitted from person to person

industrial 87 made for a factory that processes raw materials

manpower 88 use of people and time

putrefying 88 rotting and stinking

crisscross 88 make intersecting paths across

make a dent in 88 have any effect on

illumination 88 light in the building

pallets 88 straw mattresses

drone 88 M continuous (boring) hum

haze 89 M air clouded by smoke or particles

incongruous 89 not fitting

momentarily 89 for just a moment

devour 90 literally, to eat as if starving (used metaphorically)

perverse 90 awkward and unnatural

under duress 90 in response to threats or violence, i.e., not freely

hoax 90 lie; deception

undertaken 90 committed to; taken on

germinate 91 begin to grow

mixed bag 91 inconsistent collection— some good, some bad

appalled 92 shocked and dismayed

imperative 93 absolutely necessary

bunker 93 underground shelter with reinforced walls and ceiling

flat out 95 completely

migration season 96 time when birds fly south for winter / north for summer

point 96 lead position

swerves 96 suddenly changes direction

hunkered down 97 crouched down to become a smaller target and avoid attacks

expendable 98 not a significant loss; easy to abandon

rant 98 speak in a wild, passionate way

unrattled 99 calm

aloft 100 up in the air

wrap 100 end of a video-recording session

Journal and Discussion Questions

1. In this chapter Katniss echoes Gale (p. 54) in using the term *freak* (p. 87). What do you make of this?

2. How would you characterize Commander Paylor?

3. Does Collins succeed in having Katniss relate praise of herself in Chapter 6 (the meeting) and 7 (the hospital) without Katniss seeming self-centered? Explain.

4. Enumerate prior hints that Katniss has a power that she did not understand. How does Katniss recast her understanding of her relationships, once she realizes her power? What narrative results do you expect to ensue?

5. Compare the propo shoot in 8 to the one in 13.

6. Summarize the chapter from Gale's point of view.

Summary

The hovercraft carrying Katniss and her team—Gale, Cressida, Messalla, and two cameramen, Castor and Pollux—drops them in 8. Boggs leads them to a warehouse functioning as a hospital, which inspires memories of Mrs. Everdeen treating dying patients in their kitchen. Katniss tells Boggs she can't do it, and he responds that she has something that no doctor can. She meets Comannder Paylor, who invites her in. She is quickly recognized and discovers that being present and alive is in itself, an inspiration, leading to a new sense of power and recasting Snow's, Plutarch's, and Coin's responses to her.

When they leave the hospital, Boggs gets a warning of incoming bombers, and the group runs for cover, but a bomb blows Katniss off her feet. Plutarch directs them to a bunker, and Haymitch tells Katniss its important she not be spotted. Realizing that the bombers are targeting the hospital, Katniss yanks out her earpiece and heads for the roof, with Gale behind her. They find Paylor and join the attack with their weaponized bows, only to find afterwards that their film crew has joined them and captured the action. Returning to the street, they find that the hospital has been destroyed, and Katniss now realizes that Gale's views of the Capitol that led to his rants in the woods were correct. The film crew captures her rage as she threatens Snow.

Chapter 8

The First Propo; Peeta's 2nd Interview

Vocabulary

vital signs 102 critical signs of wellbeing, e.g., pulse, heartbeat, temperature

clear ... with 102 obtain permission from

shrapnel 102 fragment of a bomb, sent out from the point of explosion with great force

double vision 102 problem in which one sees everything doubled

negotiate 103 bargain

annulling 103 making an agreement invalid, as if it never existed

congenial 104 friendly

reception 104 greeting; welcome

accessible 104 able to be reached; open to communication

rocky 104 in poor condition

montage 106 footage composed of separate sections that have been selected, edited, and sequenced

superimposed 106 placed on top

relish 106 enjoyment; appreciation

indulgently 106 w/ looseningof the usual rules

on-camera talent 107 actors (as opposed to non-actors, e.g., directors, crew, etc.)

obnoxious 107 annoying

studio approach 107 using scripted material in a controlled setting

unforeseen 107 not anticipated

tolerance for 107 ability to put up with

flagrantly 107 shamelessly

give the slip 108 get away from; elude

furrowing 108 wrinkling

consensus 108 agreement of all concerned

judicious 108 guided by good judgment

exposure 108 state of being in danger

ratted out 108 told on; exposed

vengeful 108 focused on seeking revenge

cutting ... together 109 joining edited segments to make a whole

intercut 109 alternating w/

mollified 109 feeling that things have been put to rights, at least somewhat

depiction 109 portrait; representation

hollering 110 yelling loudly

transmitter 111 device that receives signals

nosedive 111 headfirst fall

relapses 112 returns to an unhealthy state

studio clips 112 footage shot in a studio

reels 113 becomes disoriented

whip up 113 encite; urge to action

put the brakes on 113 put a stop to

repudiate 114 refuse to be associated w/

Journal and Discussion Questions

1. Compare the scenes of television watching in *Mockingjay* Chapter 8 and *Catching Fire* Chapter 12, in which the Quarter Quell card was read. How are they parallel, narratively?

2. Since we "witnessed" the propo being filmed in Chapter 7, why does Collins repeat Katniss's words in this chapter?

3. Why do you think Plutarch and Fulvia do not mention Peeta?

4. Do you think Peeta is serving the Capitol, his own ends, or both in the words he directs to Katniss? Explain.

5. Summarize the chapter from Fulvia's point of view.

Summary

As Katniss sees the hospital collapse, she collapses, too, and Boggs, whose nose was broken when Gale stopped him from following them to the roof, scoops her up and carries her to the landing strip. She awakens in the hospital and is brought to Command in a wheelchair, fearing what will happen after her decisions in 8. The propo is replayed and she is impressed. The ensuing discussion clarifies for her that no one has told Coin how she ripped out her earpiece and disobeyed orders. The potential for a rift with Fulvia, who had backed the studio approach to propos, is avoided by Cressida's praise of Fulvia's idea for "We Remember" propos, narrated by Finnick and featuring dead tributes.

Wheeled back to her hospital room by Gale, Katniss sleeps for a bit and awakens to find Haymitch by her bed. He threatens her with a head shackle or an implant should she ever take her earpiece out again, and she agrees to keep it in. Finnick joins her for dinner so they can watch his first propo together, but as they are about to turn the television off, they see that Caesar Flickerman is interviewing Peeta, who looks dramatically worse, again. Caesar tells Peeta that Katniss is reportedly being used in propos by the rebels, and he responds that she can't know what's at stake. Speaking directly to her, he asks her if she trusts the people she's working with and knows what's going on, and recommends that if not, she find out. Finnick tells Katniss they should pretend they didn't see it, and when Plutarch and Fulvia come in, they do pretend, and no one mentions Peeta.

Strategy 5

Directions:
First, read the information. Then, answer the question or questions.

There are various ways that a writer can construct a multi-book series. One way is to follow a quest through many adventures to its conclusion . . . or failure . . . or its morphing into a different quest. Another is to follow different characters over a set period of time, moving between them as it serves the story. But Collins does not do either of these.

Overall, the structure of both books we've completed so far could be represented like this:

1. Katniss starts off in District 12.
2. Due to forces that are largely or completely beyond her control, Katniss ends up fighting for her life.
3. The fight ends.
4. Katniss has to deal with the consequences of both the fight *and* the way it ends.

And with all the evidence we have so far in *Mockingjay*, plus the knowledge that the narrator—since she is the narrator—survived, it's looking very much like the third book will have the same structure.

So how does Collins differentiate the three volumes. A key aspect of her approach is to **increase the challenges**: in each book, what Katniss must do is more difficult. Challenges can increase in a number of ways:

Change in the Conflicts

- the conflicts themselves can become more challenging to overcome
- the conflicts may become more frequent

Change in the Protagonist

- the protagonist may have less help or worse tools with which to face the conflicts in her path
- the protagonist can become less able to face the conflicts

Change in Both

- some combination of the above factors may be in play

But besides this, Collins also chooses to **escalate the stakes** in each book. The term *escalate the stakes* means "increasing what is at risk."

1. Explain how Collins has increased the challenges for Katniss through the trilogy thus far.
2. Explain how Collins has escalated the stakes through the trilogy thus far.
3. When you are done reading, tell whether the structural pattern shown above holds for the third book of the trilogy.

Chapter 9

Propos in District 12; The Hanging Tree; Peeta's 3rd Interview

Vocabulary

spiteful 118 mean; showing ill will; acting out of a desire to hurt

heartsick 118 lonely and grieving from disappointment in love

uncommunicative 118 closed off; intentionally isolated

mannequin 118 dummy used to display clothes in a store window

take the edge off 118 diminish; make less noticeable

brimming with 119 full of

foothold 119 secure position on which to build or from which to advance

inroads 119 progress; advances

demise 120 destruction

atrocity 120 wickedly cruel act

remnant 120 remaining part

sanctuary 121 safe place; holy place

corrupted 121 warped; twisted

stumps 121 short remains of tree trunks

variation 123 change

harmonize 124 sing a pleasing accompaniment

irrevocably 125 not able to be changed or forgotten

tryst 125 secret romantic meeting

stanza 125 section of a poem

creepiest 126 most weird and disturbing

under my belt 126 completed

dredged up 126 brought to mind

rendition 126 performance

golden 127 perfect

muddle 128 confused mess

drive ... away 128 push out of my life

thaw 128 relax; become friendlier

mishaps 128 unfortunate accidents

satellites 130 spacecraft put in orbit around the earth to collect information (spy) or improve communications

cell disintegrators 130 machines for breaking down cells

drones M 130 missiles or aircraft w/out pilots, controlled remotely

biological weapons 130 weapons using poisons or infections to harm or kill humans

expiration dates 130 times beyond which a product may not be fully effective

moral squeamishness 130 feeling that an action is not clearly right/good

intercepts 131 blocks the path of

disregard 131 ignore

underscored 131 w/ musical score added to the images for impact

barricaded 131 blocked off

infrastructure 132 basics needed for society to function, including roads, power, etc.

derailed 132 having been knocked off the tracks

water purification 132 system for making water clean and pure for drinking

peppered 133 covered with a large number of random ...

spasms 133 sudden, brief spells of emotion

in turmoil 133 in a state of utter confusion

plows forward 133 keep going, pushing through obstacles

dissemination 133 spread

reign 133 prevail; be maintained

contorts 133 twists unnaturally

privy to 133 able to observe

inseparable 134 unable to be separated; united with

Journal and Discussion Questions

1. How do the various settings in 12 affect the mood?

2. How did "The Hanging Tree" affect you?

3. After Katniss sings, Plutarch tells her she's golden and kisses her on the head. Haymitch used the same word after the first chariot ride (*HG*, p. 137), and he kissed her on the forehead after coaching her before the post-Games interview (*HG*, p. 357). Cinna kisses Katniss on the forehead just before she enters the arena for the Quarter Quell (*CF*, p. 262). What do you make of the parallels?

4. What does the repetition of the blackberry toss and quotation of Effie Trinket's tagline from *The Hunger Games* (p. 8) mean to you?

5. What does Gale believe he has figured out about Katniss's romantic interest in him? Do you agree with his analysis? Explain.

6. With all the parallels with earlier books in *Mockingjay*, one difference is that Gale never calls Katniss *Catnip*. What do you make of this?

7. What does Plutarch's monologue on the way back to District 13 say about him?

8. How does Plutarch's response to Beetee's success relate to the reactions of others in the room? What does this suggest about Plutarch?

9. Write a news story that gives an objective report of the broadcast battle and includes brief quotations from Plutarch and Haymitch.

10. What do you make of Peeta's words to Katniss in this 3rd interview?

11. Compare and contrast the three interviews.

12. What do you think will happen to Peeta now? Explain why you think as you do.

13. How would you classify the ending of this chapter: cliffhanger, shocker, or something else? Explain.

14 Summarize the chapter from Cressida's point of view.

Summary

Too upset about Peeta to sleep, Katniss is released from the hospital in the morning, and spends the day waiting for someone to mention Peeta's appearance, but no one does. Since Gale is busy with Beetee, Katniss takes Finnick to the woods, where they discuss the lack of response. Finnick suggests that Gale may be waiting to speak to her privately, but when he walks her back to her room after dinner and she asks him what's going on, he doesn't respond. After her family is asleep, she gets the pearl and clutches it while she reviews Peeta's words, wonders if Peeta actually knows something and why no one has mentioned it, and realizes that while he's been trying to protect her, she's made things worse for him.

In the morning she confronts Gale, who asks why she didn't say something, and when she responds that he's the one that should have, he tells her that everyone worried that seeing it would make her sick. She confirms this, but counters that Gale lying to her for Coin makes her sicker. When his communicuff beeps, she suggests that he's spying on her for Coin, and he first looks hurt, then angry. Katniss reflects that she's sick of people lying to her.

Cressida announces that her plans are unscripted interviews with Katniss and Gale in 12. On the hovercraft, Plutarch shows Katniss that the rebels—inspired by the propos—have gained control of 3 and 11 and are making inroads elsewhere and Katniss surmises that Gale hasn't told him and Coin that she saw Peeta's second interview. Cressida leads them back to Katniss's old house in the Seam, then Gale's, and then they retrace the steps he took to lead the remainder of 12 to safety by the lake. Pollux, whom Katniss has learned is an Avox, is sitting next to her, and she shows him a mockingjay and whistles a few notes to demonstrate. Pollux then takes a turn, and then writes "Sing" in the dirt, asking if Katniss will demonstrate their capabilities. She chooses to sing "The Hanging Tree" and recalls when she learned it from her father as a child and was interrupted by her mother who was horrified at teaching little children the song. She then explains the meaning of the song. Realizing that she has been filmed and that Pollux is crying from some awful memory, she stands still until Cressida says "cut." Plutarch, impressed, tells her she's golden and kisses the top of her head.

Cressida next takes them to Gale's and Katniss's old hunting rendezvous. As Katniss recalls their happy days, she wonders if she really desires to drive him away? She repeats their old blackberry trick from *HG*, and Gale responds, and they start to warm up as they recount their hunting adventures. Finally, Cressida takes them to the site of the destroyed bakery and asks Katniss to addres Peeta. She tells him that both 12 and his family are gone and asks how he could ask for a cease-fire. Turning to the remains of the gallows, Cressida asks if either Gale or Katniss had ever been tortured. Gale pulls of his shirt to show where he was lashed, while Katniss walks away and heads to the Victor's Village, claiming she needs to get something for her mother. She collects bottles and jars, and is startled by Gale, who recalls that Katniss kissed him in the kitchen, and tells her that he's figured out that he's only appealing to her when he's in pain.

As they fly home, Plutarch mourns for the high tech weapons of yesteryear, and Katniss goes to bed without dinner, and naps in the supply closet after breakfast. After lunch she meets Boggs in the hall, and he tells her she's wanted in Command. Finnick explains that Beetee thinks he can break into the Capitol newsfeed, and he's about to try it out. As the Capitol seal appears, she sees President Snow at a podium, with Peeta sitting beside him, looking disoriented, frightening Katniss. He speaks about the damage the rebels have caused and the need for a cease-fire until, suddenly, Beetee breaks in, confusing Peeta, who nevertheless tries to keep going. Plutarch is delighted, but Finnick, Katniss, and Haymitch are terrified for Peeta. Snow returns and decries the rebel attempts to interrupt the news feed and asks Peeta if he has any words for Katniss. With an incredible effort, he warns that those in 13 will be "dead by morning," and as the broadcast is cut, they hear Peeta being hit and see his blood on the tile floor.

Writer's Forum 1 — Writing a Ballad

Directions:
First, read the information. Then, answer the question or questions.

Ballads are narrative folk songs that may be serious or humorous. They often tell the dramatic story of a romance, a conflict, or the adventures of an outlaw hero. Katniss's father taught her ballads (p. 376), and "The Hanging Tree" was evidently in that category. We need this identification to know how it should sound, as well as how to interpret it. It's possible that Collins intended ballads of Panem to differ from the ballads that we know, but because there are no other ballads in the trilogy, we need to use the genre conventions of the ballads we know as a jumping off point.

The characters in ballads are flat. The main character is generally introduced in the first lines, using a name (e.g., Lord Randall, Sweet William) or a brief **stock phrase** (a pretty fair miss, a shepherd's daughter, a rich Dutchman), but there is no further character development. There's often an identification of the setting—either time (on the very first day of the year, a May morning) or place (Nottingham, at his castle gate), but then the focus turns to the action. Additional characters or settings are introduced in just a few words as they come into the story. You can infer from this information, that many ballads deal in stereotypes: parents and children, sisters and brother, outlaws and heroes, men and women in love. Ballads are almost always told in the third person, though they often include dialogue. There is no comment by the speaker, who is an outside observer: the focus is squarely on what is being told, not the teller.

The organization and structure of ballads has some special attributes. Often, ballads have verses, with no chorus. But the verses may have **repetend** (repeated material) that has a similar effect to a chorus. Here, for example, are the first two verses of "The Cruel Sister":

> There lived an honest man and true,
>   O might I follow thee!
> And daughters had but only two;
>   So dupest thou not me!

> The younger bright as is the sun,
>   O might I follow thee!
> But black as dirt the elder one;
>   So dupest thou not me!

You can see that the second and fourth lines are identical in the two verses.

Repetition within a line is also used: ballads have both phrases that are repeated identically, one after the other, as well as **incremental repetition**, in which material is repeated with minor changes: This stanza from "Lady Maisry" includes both:

> "O saddle me the black, the black,
>   Or saddle me the brown;
> O saddle me the swiftest steed
>   That ever rode through a town."

In the first line, the words "the black" are repeated exactly. But the words "saddle me" make up the central element of three slightly different phrases.

Many poems that have stress patterns called feet, like iambic pentameter. These poems are analyzed using both stresses (accents) and the number of syllables in a line: they are **accentual-syllabic verse**. Ballads, in contrast, are **accentual verse**, in which only the number of stresses per line (not the number of syllables) is counted. This makes sense when you consider that ballads were sung before they were ever written down: the stresses match up with the downbeat and other strong beats in the musical meter, with more or fewer syllables fitted in between, as needed. Even in versions with different words and numbers of syllables, many of the same syllables are stressed, and this make sense because the stresses

derive from the natural stresses from speaking the words. To demonstrate how the words fit the musical meter, here are two versions of a verse from the same basic song: Version 1 is from "Lady Isabel and the Elf Knight"; Version 2, from "Pretty Polly."

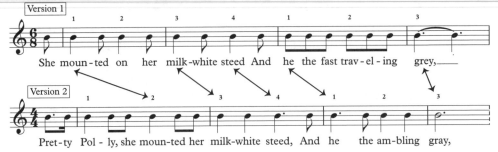

The versions have different numbers of syllables and different meters. But the syllables that are emphasized (numbered above) always fall on the beats of the measures that receive the most stress, and any other syllables are fitted in between. This provides us some guidance for how we might read "The Hanging Tree," though it is only one possibility

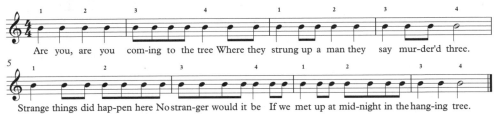

Ballads are usually written in two- or four-lines **stanzas**, and this is probably connected to their rhyme schemes. There are three rhyme schemes that ballads often use. The rhyme scheme used in "The Cruel Sister," *a b a b* is very common. In this scheme, the first and third lines rhyme, and the second and fourth lines rhyme. The rhyme of lines one and three is made clearer when the verse is written in four lines. Another common scheme is *x a x a* (no rhyme in the first and third line; rhyme in the second and fourth). These ballads may be rendered on only two lines. An alternative is *monorhyme* in which a single rhyme is used in every line of the stanza: *a a a a*.

1. Which conventional elements of a ballad does "The Hanging Tree" exhibit? How does it differ from a conventional ballad? Offer an explanation for this.

2. Analyze the meaning of "The Hanging Tree," with attention to grammar and punctuation based solely on the text. Does the meaning you derive match Katniss's interpretation? If yes, since the meaning is indicated by the lyrics, why did Collins spell it out? If not, how does Katniss's interpretation alter, take liberties with, or force a reading that the lyrics don't uphold and why would Collins do this?

3. Rewrite "The Hanging Tree" as a more conventional ballad, using the features explained above. Feel free to make up details that are in keeping with the lyrics as Collins wrote them. As you do so, check to make sure that your ballad fits both the original and Katniss's interpretation as best you can, but can be understood without commentary. Write a short essay explaining the decisions you made as you created your ballad. Optional: Set your ballad to music.

Vocabulary

Look at each group of words. Tell why it is important in the story.

1. incineration, decomposition, carrion, firestorm
2. pox, infertile, breeding stock, genetic diversity
3. imprinted, get with the program, clockwork precision
4. weaponry, retinal, DNA, scans, metal detectors
5. fashion accessory, incendiary, shaft
6. supply chain, republic, centralized government
7. montage, superimposed, on-camera talent
8. satellites, cell disintegrators, drones, biological weapons

Essay Topics

1. What evidence in Part I suggests that the Games are still not really over?

2. Katniss has fought for her life in all three books. How are the differences in the fighting meaningful? Use the Choice Analysis Tool (pp. 42–3) to aid your explanation.

3. When Boggs tells the group in response to Fulvia's praise of Gale's looks, that no one should expect Katniss and him to be impressed because they just saw Finnick Odair in his underwear (p. 82), Collins does not supply a response for Gale. What do you think he was thinking? Why? Why do you think Collins chose not to have him speak?

4. How would you characterize Fulvia?

5. Do you think Plutarch speaks for all the rebels when he lays out the plan for a new form of government if they beat the Capitol forces? Explain your thoughts.

6. How has Collins used sensory detail in Part I of *Mockingjay*? Provide examples.

7. Katniss mentions "trying to sort out what is true and what is false" (p. 4). How is this a key consideration in the trilogy so far?

8. How have Prim and Mrs. Everdeen changed since the first book of the trilogy?

9. How does Katniss's experience in the hospital fit into the greater pattern of her experience with health care of various types?

10. What is the inciting incident for *Mockingjay*? How does it relate to the inciting incidents for *The Hunger Games* and *Catching Fire*?

11. What meaning do you take from Katniss's statement at the end of Chapter 6, "Cinna, it seems, has thought of everything"?

12. What do you think is the significance of the way Collins phrased what Katniss sees in Haymitch's eyes while watching the third interview with Peeta (p. 133)?

13. Rank the top 10 characters in terms of their power, identifying the facts that support your assessment

14. Explain how you adjusted your reading to account for different sections of the text.

15. What is the reversal in Act I of *Mockingjay*? Explain how you identified it.

16. If you were the author of this story, what would happen next? How would you develop the plot?

Chapter 10

**PART II: "THE ASSAULT"
District 13 Goes
on Lockdown**

Vocabulary

counterproductive 138 have the opposite effect of that desired

environmental 138 effecting the surroundings, including plant and animal life

radiation 138 emission of particles and gamma rays during nuclear decay

incalculable 138 unable to be estimated (w/ the implication that they will be enormous

compound 138 group of buildings that fulfill a particular function

counterstrike 138 counterattack having the form of a strike, i.e., a sudden, surprise military response

acceptable risks 138 risks decided by the government to be okay to take, on behalf of citizens who have no voice in the decision

subtleties of irony 138 clever, indirect way of expressing oneself when using irony

exempted 138 excused from participating

congregate 138 come together at a meeting place

quarantine 139 period of isoloation to control the spread of disease

contagion 139 being in a state in which they could infect others w/ the virus

outbreak 139 arrival and spread of a disease

pulsating 139 creating a throbbing sound

fear-inducing 139 causing fear

permeate 139 spread through

cavern 139 a large cave

gone astray 140 gotten lost

hewn 140 carved

setback 140 minor interruption of plans; hitch

downgraded 140 reduced in importance

dire 140 horribly urgent

slow on the uptake 140 a long time in understanding the point

discernible 142 recognizable

latter 142 most recently mentioned of several items

inward 143 towards the center

indiscriminately 143 in a manner that isn't planned or thoughtful

scruff of the neck 144 back of the neck

visualize 144 imagine

resentfully 145 w/ feelings of injury for having been treated badly

exemplary 146 setting an outstanding example

evacuation 146 act of leaving a dangerous place to seek safety

televised 146 transmitted via television

resonates M 146 is filled with an echoing sound

innermost 146 deepest inside

marrow 146 soft material in the cavities of bones that create blood cells

disorientation of 146 confusion about location and direction caused by

generator 146 backup power source

croons 147 hums or sings softly

orientation 147 introduction

gloom 147 partial darkness

vault 147 large, underground room

stampede 147 panicked rush of people, who have lost concern for anything but their own safety

wanly 147 weakly

emits 149 gives off; is the source of

dank 149 cold, damp, and musty-smelling

deterioration 150 appearance of having been more abused and unwell than before

break 151 shatter; destroy; make unable to function

Journal and Discussion Questions

1. What is the significance of Katniss's comparison of herself to an Avox?
2. How does Katniss use visualization in this chapter?
3. Describe a Level Five security drill and tell how it differs from a Level Two drill?
4. What evidence suggests that Plutarch is correct in predicting the effects of Katniss's behavior in the bunker? What does this tell you about him?
5. Katniss's uses several similes and metaphors in this chapter. Identify the figures of speech. What you think Collins intended? Did she succeed?
6. Compare and contrast President Coin's initial reaction to the question of whether Peeta intended a warning, her explanation as they wait in the bunker, and her response after the first bomb hits.
7. How does the theme of debt return in this chapter?
8. Assess why Plutarch used the term *setback* to describe what happened to Peeta. Then assess the impact it had on Katniss.
9. What do you think is the significance of Prim "crooning" to Buttercup? Support your thoughts with examples.

10. Katniss identifies Peeta's internal struggle to convey the warning to District 13. Predict what this struggle might indicate and how it might play out.
11. What is your response to the last sentence of the chapter? Explain why you think as you do.
12. Summarize the chapter from Prim's point of view.

Summary

Katniss's inability to voice her grief at seeing Peeta beaten contrasts with the uproar in the room as those who don't know Peeta attempt to parse his words. Haymitch interrupts to interpret, but struggles to convince the others and calls on Katniss to support his view. She does, and Haymitch reiterates to President Coin that they must prepare for an attack. After consideration, in which she takes multiple factors into account, combined with the fact that a security drill is overdue, she orders a Level Five lockdown—a more serious drill than has occured since Katniss's arrival in 13, one of which she was oblivious to, stlll being in intensive care, and the other of which she sat out in the laundry room.

The Level Five drill commences with ear-piercing sirens, which—rather than inspiring chaos—lead to an orderly movement to caverns deep within the earth, where the technology accounts for every citizen, and the space is prepared for a long stay. As Katniss moves to the E section, Plutarch approaches her. Acknowledging her concern with Peeta's "setback," he warns her that her behavior will have a profound effect on the others in the bunker, missing the sarcasm of her response. Katniss reads the bunker protocol, and goes to the Supply Station, where a line immediately forms, making her wonder if Plutarch has read things correctly. After unpacking the supplies, Katniss sits down to wait, and her mother arrives, asking about Prim, and indicating that Prim left the hospital 10 minutes before she herself did. Katniss realizes that Prim must have gone after Buttercup, and Katniss loses her sense of leadership, rushing to the door, shoving people aside, and shouting for the guards who are almost done closing the door in preparation for sealing it shut to stop, and sticks her hand in the remaining crack, yelling her sister's name out into the stairwell. Prim's response and footsteps are heard, and the guards open the door a bit wider until Prim, holding Buttercup, and Gale, carrying prized Everdeen family possessions, appear and enter.

Katniss tries to live up to Plutarch's admonishment as she crosses from the now-closed door back to her family's assigned space. She sees that—along with medical supplies brought from District 12 and her hunting bag—Gale rescued the family plant book, her parents' wedding photo, and the special items from her drawer: the locket, and the silver parachute with the spile and pearl tied into it. The sirens end, and Coin goes on the public address system to praise the evacuation, and explaining that Peeta's possible reference to an attack in a televised program, with the first bomb hitting just after her speech. The lights go out, and Katniss huddles with Prim, Buttercup, and her mother, while Prim tentatively identifies a bunker bomb, but is unable to discern whether it is nuclear or not.

Mrs. Everdeen expresses gratitude for Peeta's warning, leading Katniss to reflect that Peeta seemed to be undergoing an internal struggle in order to enunciate the warning. Her thoughts are interrupted by Coin's voice, now explicitly acknowledging District 13's debt to Peeta, and informing citizens that the bomb were *not* nuclear, but that further bombing is expected.

As they go about the mundane tasks of organizing the space and preparing for sleep, Katniss appreciates having time with Prim and realizes that she has not been watching over her due to her intense focus on her own affairs. Prim reveals that she expects to be trained as a doctor—something that wouldn't have been possible in 12. Katniss tells Prim about Peeta's worsening condition and her expectation that he is probably being murdered. Prim holds her and tellls her that she doesn't think Peeta will be killed because if he was, President Snow would no longer have the power to hurt Katniss. Recalling Johanna Mason's comment (*CF*) that she was beyond being hurt because there was no one left that she loves, Katniss realizes that Prim is right. She asks what Prim thinks they'll do to him, and she replies, "Whatever it takes to break you."

Chapter 11

Vocabulary

consumes 152 uses all of one's attention

shock waves 152 sudden, dramatic changes of air pressure from exploding bombs

socialization 153 iteraction w/ others beyond one's family

tedium 153 lack of change; boredom

petty 153 spiteful

tailspin 153 state of panic w/ frantic action

unendurable 154 heartbreaking

brownouts 154 partial blackouts, w/ dimming or cutting of only some electricity

fissures 154 cracks

lure 155 tempt someone to go

broken out . . . 157 opened and started using . . .

stimulant 157 method to heighten awareness and mental capability

dominant 158 most powerful

distastefully 158 w/ disgust

made him tick 158 defined or motivated him

plunking 158 dropping w/out trying to be gentle mm

minimal 158 very little

poultry 159 domesticated birds, including chickens, ducks, geese, and turkeys

jutted 160 stuck out from the main section of something

superficial 160 minimal

wilted 161 droopy

wired 161 on edge

merciful 162 kind; humane

entails 163 results in

sleeping . . . off 164 sleeping until the effects of (a drug or alcohol) wear off

waxen 164 pale

sedative 164 drug that brings on sleep

lost it 164 was overcome by mental imbalance; lost control of himself

in reruns 164 showing old footage again w/out any new material

Journal and Discussion Questions

1. What breaks Katniss?
2. How does the attack on District 13 play out? What seems to be its purpose?
3. Do you find Katniss's Crazy Cat metaphor effective? Explain your response.
4. Do you find Collins's explanation in *MJ* for why Finnick looked at Katniss quizzically when Peeta almost died in *CF* (p. 282) believable? Explain.
5. Is it believable that rope tying keeps Finnick and Katniss from mental collapse? Explain why you think as you do.
6. Why is the planned propo important?
7. Why do you think Collins chose to have Gale suspect a romantic relationship between Katniss and Finnick?
8. Do you think the bombings are the assault mentioned in the part title?
9. Predict whether the rescue mission will succeed, and at what cost.
10. Summarize the chapter from Finnick's point of view.

Summary

Over the next three days, four more bunker bombs are dropped, and Katniss invents the game Crazy Cat, providing entertainment for others and herself with a metaphor for her situation vis-à-vis Peeta. The understanding that Peeta is being tortured specifically with the intent to incapacitate her starts to break Katniss, and the night that she comes up with the metaphor, she seeks out Finnick, whom, she realizes, is in the same situation with regard to Annie. He loans her his piece of rope, with which he continually ties and unties knots in order to distract himself and keep a grip on reality, and Katniss passes the night with it.

The next day, Coin lifts the lockdown, and citizens are assigned to new housing due to the damage the bombs inflicted. As Katniss is heading to her family's new quarters, Boggs pulls her aside and takes her to a duplicate of the Command room, where Coin order a new propo to establish the damage, the unimpaired function of 13's military, and that the Mockingjay is alive and well. As they prepare to film, Haymitch asks what benefit came from Peeta's warning, and Katniss realizes that Gale and Prim would have died but for Peeta. As they head to the ruins of the old Justice Building, they come upon dozens of the same roses that were used to celebrate Katniss's and Peeta's victory. Katniss knows that it's designed to unhinge her, and it does. She is unable to complete the propo, and breaks down crying, with Haymitch coming to comfort her until she's given a sedative. He is there when she awakens and reports a rescue mission for Peeta and Annie is underway, led by Boggs and staffed by volunteers, the first of whom was Gale.

Writer's Forum 2

Writing an Extended Metaphor

We have identified *metaphor* as a comparision in which two things that are, in fact, different are equated. In a simple metaphor, there is usually a limited comparison. Whereas *simile* uses *like* or *as* in the comparison, metaphor makes the comparison more direct. An *extended metaphor* draws multiple points of comparison. An example occurs in a speech by the character Jacques in Shakespeare's play *As You Like It* II, vi:

> All the world's a stage
> And all the men and women merely players;
> They have their exits and their entrances,
> And one man in his time plays many parts . . .

Shakespeare begins with one metaphor: a comparison of the world to a stage. He then takes it a step further by comparing people to actors, and birth to entrances and death to exits and the different roles we have at various stages of life to different acting roles. But by the time he's laid out the relationship of people to players, we can see where he's going. He no longer has to give the first term of the comparison: he doesn't mention birth, death, or—at this point in the speech—the roles that people play in various stages of life. The metaphor is clear enough that we can figure these things out. The audience being able to interpret the metaphor is an important element.

To write an extended metaphor, you need to think of two things with multiple points of comparison and then decide how to play it out for your audience.

1. Explain the extended metaphor of Crazy Cat to Katniss in your own words.

2. Write an extended metaphor using one of these pairs of items, or a pair of your own:

   a. books and friends

   b. the mind and a house

   c. imagination and a vacation

Chapter 12

Vocabulary

stilled 166 quieted; stopped moving

anesthetize 166 remove feelings and memories (figurative)

divert 167 distract

ebbs 167 fades away; diminishes

decoy 168 event designed to distract

open up 168 talk about topics publicly for the first time

tapestry 171 a rich, complicated tale, made up of many strands (figurative)

bottomless 171 unending

power plays 171 tactics designed to increase one's own power and influence

slip 171 failure

incest 171 having sexual relations with one's child, sibling, grandchild or other close member of one's birth family

back-stabbing 171 betraying and/or attacking one's friends and allies

blackmail 171 seeking money in exchange for not revealing illegal or immoral actions

arson 171 setting fires on purpose

recrimination 171 accusations and blame

ascension 171 rise to power

shellfish 171 seafood with shells

viruses 171 agents of infection

aorta 171 the body's main blood vessel

antidotes 172 cures for poisons

allegations 172 accusations

displaced 172 forced by war to leave home

cut 172 stop filming

leverage against me 173 influence he could use to change my opinion

salacious 173 treating serious matters as the subject of gossip

techno 173 (abbrev) technology

coup 173 notable tactical success

relinquishing 173 giving up voluntarily

insiders 174 people w/ access to a group's most private information

knockout gas 174 substance that makes people unconscious or unable to act

power failure 174 loss of power/electricity, resulting in outages

detonation 174 explosion

disruption 174 interruption

sideswiped 175 hit at an angle and not w/ full force

gurney 175 stretcher with wheels

bedraggled 175 dirty and messy

indivisible 176 not able to be separated

giddiness 176 lighthearted excitement

cold collar 178 medical device that fits the neck and provides hours of cold therapy

Journal and Discussion Questions

1. How did Collins prepare readers to make a great deal of meaning out of the two-word sentence "Hands stilled." (p. 166)?
2. How did learning Haymitch's story affect your view of him and why?
3. What information that you already knew is recapped in this chapter? Why?
4. Finnick mentions President Snow's first name for the first time. Research it to figure out why you think Collins chose it, and explain your thoughts..
5. Summarize Finnick's revelations.
6. Did you realize, as you read Katniss's predictions for how her reunion with Peeta would go, that Collins was setting you up? Explain what you thought.
7. Predict what will happen next.
8. Summarize the chapter from Haymitch's point of view.

Summary

Realizing that she might lose both Gale and Peeta in a single day, Katniss begs Haymitch for something to do to contribute to the rescue mission. After consulting Plutarch, Haymitch offers Katniss and Finnick an opportunity to both get the necessary post-bombing footage as well as provide a decoy for the rescue. Katniss recounts how she met Peeta and explains that his suffering has removed her reservations about doing "whatever it takes" to destroy the Capitol. Finnick tells how President Snow sold him and how he was paid in secrets, and then proceeds to recount those secrets, first about anyone with power, and finally about President Snow, who—Finnick reveals—has used poison throughout his career to rid his path of allies and rivals alike. Snow employed an antidote that allowed him to drink the poison, but it left him with mouth sores, and he wears roses to cover the smell of blood. Katniss asks if Haymitch was sold as well, but since Snow had killed everyone Haymitch loved in response to his force field trick, there wasn't any leverage left. Beetee explains the outline of the plan to Finnick and Katniss, but Haymitch interrupts to say that the rescue team is back. They spot Johanna Mason unconscious and Gale in surgery for a wound. Annie throws herself into Finnick's arms, making Katniss jealous of their certainty. Boggs tells Katniss that Peeta has awoken. Daydreaming about their blissful reunion, she runs to embrace him, but his hands close around her throat.

Chapter 13

Katniss Recovers; Beetee & Gale; Delly & Peeta

Vocabulary

chafes 178 rubs, making sore

disembodied 178 heard over a loud speaker, thus lacking any physical presence

spinal cord 178 nerves and tissue enclosed in the spine and connecting to the brain

airway 178 trachea, through which air passes from mouth/nose to lungs

veins 178 tubes that carry blood to the heart

arteries 178 tubes that carry blood from the heart

allayed 178 put to rest; ended

larynx 178 structure holding the vocal cords

conditioning 180 training to behave in a certain way

long-term storage 181 memory storage for recall in the distant future)

rehabilitation 181 efforts to restore someone to mental health

tampered w/ 182 damaged or corrupted

caustically 182 sarcastically; bitterly

restraint 183 self-control

confined to bed 183 made to stay in bed as part of medical treatment

inherited 184 received from previous generations

level head 184 calm, reasonable approach

subterranean 184 underground

litter 185 make untidy w/ a bunch of items

corkboard 185 material designed for mounting papers w/ thumbtacks or push-pins

harmonious 185 pleasant and free of disagreements

fundamental 185 basic

psychology 185 scientific study of the human mind and human behavior

offspring 185 children

unacceptable 186 beyond what can be tolerated

hostility 186 feelings of opposition and antagonism

go ballistic 186 fly into a rage

waylaid 186 stopped in my path

drab 187 dull, uninteresting

one-way glass 188 material that appears to be a mirror on one side, but can be seen through on the other

lucid 188 like he's in conscious control

Journal and Discussion Questions

1. Analyze the shift in roles that has taken place between Katniss and Prim.
2. What makes Plutarch's view of Peeta's situation so different from Katniss's?
3. Examine the relationship between Katniss's two encounters with Gale in this chapter.
4. Why do you think Collins has Prim suggest that Katniss and Buttercup keep each other company?
5. Explain Katniss's view of the weapons Beetee and Gale are developing.
6. Characterize Delly Cartwright.
7. What does it mean that Peeta thinks Katniss is a mutt?
8. Summarize the chapter from Delly's point of view.

Summary

Ordered not to speak, Katniss shivers in a cold collar, having learned that her body will recover, but afraid she is losing her mind. She recalls that Boggs knocked Peeta out, saving her life and notes how unusual it is that both she and Haymitch could be caught off guard. Prim comes in to care for her, and Plutarch, Beetee, and Haymitch to provide an update on Peeta. Beetee explains that Peeta has been hijacked, i.e., had a type of conditioning that uses tracker jacker venom to invest memories with fear and doubt, so that Peeta now sees Katniss as a threat. Plutarch reveals that there is no known instance of rehabilitation from hijacking adding that they don't yet know the extent of memories that have been tampered with. Gale disobeys orders to stop by and kiss her forehead.

When Katniss is discharged from the hospital, Prim takes Katniss to their new quarters, but Katniss heads to Special Defense, where she finds Beetee and Gale applying Gale's animal trap psychology to traps for humans, reaching a point that Katniss feels is beyond the pale, which Gale resents, telling her that they're folowing the same rulebook Snow followed when he hijacked Peeta. Katniss hurriedly departs, only to be waylaid by Haymitch, who tells her that Peeta's team is screening 12 residents to find someone innocuous and unconnected with Katniss to visit with Peeta. They choose Delly Cartwright, who knew Peeta from preschool years. She enters Peeta's room and attempts to keep the conversation pleasant, but when he learns of the fire in District 12, he yells that Katniss is a mutt and a liar. Katniss concludes that Peeta is "irretrievable" and asks to be sent away, so Plutarch decides to send her to District 2.

Writer's Forum 3   Writing a Definition

Directions:
First, read the information. Then, answer the question or questions.

A **definition** is a complete, succinct explication of a concept, term, or idea. A definition attempts to get at the essential nature of the thing being defined, either by direct statement or by showing the thing in a revealing context. A good definition is clear, exact, and complete. It is helpful in letting people know if they are really talking about the same thing.

Definitions answer the following questions, as appropriate:

- What is the name of the thing being defined? How are you going to consistently refer to it?
- What categories or groups can it be placed in? or What kind of thing is it?
- What are its essential attributes?
- How does it work?
- How did/does it originate or arise?
- What does it do/accomplish?
- What are its functions?
- What are examples of it?
- What are some things that might be mistaken for it, but are not really it, and how can they be distinguished from the real thing?
- What is its value or usefulness?
- How is it similar to and different from similar (and more familiar) terms?

Some words that you might incorporate include:

- for example
- e.g.
- specifically
- as
- for instance
- such as
- like
- consists of

1. Write a definition of *hijacking.*

Chapter 14

District 2 with Gale and a Death Trap

Vocabulary

impenetrable 192 impossible to enter; unable to be breached
significant 192 important
cavernous 192 shaped like a cavern
slabs 192 large, thick layers
mudslides 193 flows of mud down slopes, creating a path of destruction
banks 193 set of similar or related items grouped in rows
barracks 193 quarters for soldiers
hangar 193 parking garage for aircraft
fortress 193 protected and difficult-to-penetrate structure
inhabitants 193 people who live in a place
quarry 193 deep pit from which stone is dug
funneled 193 moved along a career path by narrowing options
stonecutters 194 workers who remove stone from quarries or who shape it for use
mental clarity 194 clear understanding

programmed 195 brainwashed so as to act in a predetermined way
dubious 195 questionable; not to be relied on
technological expertise 196 extensive knowledge of and skill in the use of technology
relieve ... of ... 196 take away ... from ...
hazardous 197 dangerous
kindling 197 twigs and sticks used to start a fire
unblinking 198 w/ eyes wide open
virile 200 manly
persistent 200 stubborn; trying continually
virtual tour 200 tour carried out using 3-D maps on a computer or handheld device
fortifications 200 defenses to help prevent attack
innovative 201 new and original
blueprints 202 printed building plans, showing layouts and locations
rudimentary 202 fundamental; basic

Journal and Discussion Questions

1. Explain how the content of Chapter 14 grows out of Chapters 3, 9, and 13.
2. Compare and contrast Plutarch's and Haymitch's phone reports to Katniss on Peeta's condition.
3. Discuss whether Katniss is using Gale when she kisses him.
4. Compare and contrast Peeta's and Gale's descriptions of realizing that Katniss was "the one" for him?
5. Write a brief history of District 2 in chronological order.
6. Do you think Prim's suggestion for Peeta's treatment has promise? Explain why you think as you do.
7. What do you think of Gale's plan for the Nut? Explain why you think as you do.
8. Summarize the chapter from Gale's point of view..

Summary

Katniss has been in District 2 for two weeks and provides background on its history and relationship with the Capitol, and more specifically, the history of the Nut, as the mountain that houses the underground military stronghold of the district is called. While the rebels control the outer villages, the Nut, with fortified entrances, is controlled by the Capitol, the last holdout against the district takeovers. Katniss, forbidden to fight, does this and that to help the rebel cause, and is frequently relocated for safety. Boggs, who came to District 2 with Katniss believes that the rescue was too easy and that the Capitol was planning on hand-delvering Peeta with the hope and plan that he would murder Katniss. Away from 13, Katniss is more aware of what she's lost, and tries to convince herself that whatever she had with Peeta is lost forever, despite Plutarch's falsely cheerful reports and Prim's suggestion for hijacking Peeta back. Katniss converts her pain into her desire to kill Snow.

Beetee and Gale arrive to tackle the problem of the Nut. Gale had seen Peeta and believes he can't compete with him, he kisses Katniss, and she empties her mind, not realizing that, for Gale, this nullifies the kiss. They talk about when Gale realized she was special to him. The next day the brains from 13 tackle the Nut, after an introduction from Lyme, the commander in 2 and a victor. Gale asks whether they need to take the Nut or merely disable it. He suggests using avalanches to completely block it, in effect nullifying its command center, but at the same time, killing everyone inside.

Strategy 6 Analyzing Choices

Directions:
First, read the information. Then, answer the question or questions.

Here is the 4-part Choice Analysis Tool to use in understanding choices in *Mockingjay*. Part 1 is for analyzing the situation, Part 2 for analyzing motivation (why people make the choices they do), Part 3 for analyzing the decision maker's access to reliable information, and Part 4 for analyzing the finality of the choice.

1. Use the Choice Analysis Tool to characterize Katniss's choice to be the Mockingjay in Chapter 3 of *Mockingjay*.
2. Offer a suggestion for where hijacking should fit into the Choice Analysis Tool and explain why you believe it fits there.

PART 1—TYPES OF CHOICES

Free Choice (Voluntary)

A decision with no limitations or constraint from anyone or anything

- A *pet owner* decides to name her gerbil *Wally*, rather than *Rudolfus*.

Offer (Voluntary)

A decision in which some alternative possibility with no strings or pressure is considered and freely chosen

- A *commuter* accepts a ride from a neighbor headed in the same direction rather than walk.

Constrained Choice (Voluntary within the constrained circumstances)

A decision in which there is some limitation caused by resources or the situation (such as money, time, other peoples' taste), but no threat

- A *teen* watches a movie online instead of going to the theatre. ($/time/transportation)

Bargain (Voluntary)

A decision in which two or more people come to a mutual agreement without threat, and with or without compromise

- A *man* agrees to lunch with a colleague who has a 2-for-1 deal at an expensive restaurant on the understanding that they will split the bill.

Choice w/ Spelled-Out Consequences (Voluntary)

A decision in which choices are curtailed by the consequences, which may be arbitrary, but do not violate the decision-maker's rights and are presented as fact, not threat

- A *woman* having a garage sale wants to sell a CD for $8. A shopper says she won't spend more than $6 for it.

Exploitive Choice (Either Voluntary-Under-the-Circumstances or Involuntary)

A choice is offered that takes advantage of a power differential and the fact that the chooser is not in a position to bargain.

- A *person* with no unemployment benefits and no other job prospects is offered a job for wages that are less that the value of his labor.

Coerced Choice (Either Voluntary-Under-the-Circumstances or Involuntary)

A decision that is influenced by a credible threat, with the consequence for non-compliance being unwelcome and violating the coerced person's rights/freedom.

- A *person* is told by a blackmailer to pay a certain sum or the illegal thing the person did will be shared with the police.

Terrorized Choice (Either Voluntary-Under-the-Circumstances or Involuntary)

A decision that is not only influenced by a credible threat that violates the person's rights and is unwelcome, but is made more credible by the fact that harm has or is currently being caused or physical force is being used, so that the person's rights/freedom are already violated in unwelcome ways.

- A *person* being held hostage is commanded to rob a bank or lose his/her life.

PART 2—MOTIVATIONS/INTENTIONS/DESIRES

Seeking a good for oneself

Life

Food and Water
Shelter
Safety
Sleep
Health/Healthcare
Equality

Liberty

Freedom from coercion and terrorism
Rational, predictable, fair, honest treatment by the state
Justice
Self-Direction

Happiness

Become Educated
Achieve Accomplishments
(e.g., Attain Physical Prowess, Succeed in a Career, Attain
and Exercise Authority)
Acquire and Own Property
Gain Status Corresponding to Accomplishments
Enjoy Love/Friendship/Family
Express one's Feelings
Create Beauty
Reach a Satisfied Emotional State
(e.g., Take a Vacation, Go for a Walk in Nature)
Enjoy Entertainment
Build Community

Seeking a good for specific other person

Same as good for self, more or less

Seeking a good for the community

Same as good for self, more or less

Seeking a Theoretical Good

Doing the right thing by practicing a virtue or following a rule, law, or
belief
Keeping a promise or fulfilling another type of obligation or responsibility

*(Any of the above can be carried out to excess/immoderately, illegally,
or with disregard for others or to the detriment of others; some can be
carried out inadequately.)*

PART 3—INFORMATION LEVEL AND AWARENESS

Level of Information

No Information
Partial Information
Complete Information

Awareness of Level of Information

Aware
Partially Aware
Unaware
Mistaken in awareness of level

Quality of Information

True
False
Misinformation
Lies
Invalid Conclusions
Wishful Thinking

PART 4—EXTENT OF CHOICE

Final Choice

Non-Final Choice

Choice Made in Stages
Retracted Choice
Revised Choice

Strategy 6, cont.

Chapter 15

Vocabulary

neutrally 204 unbiased; w/out taking sides
reflect on 205 consider
coerced 205 persuaded by force or threats
antiaircraft 207 for attacking enemy aircraft
insignificant 207 unimportant (by comparison)
shafts 207 tubes for carrying a substance (e.g., air)
disgorged 208 delivered; spit out (figurative)
retaliate 209 attack in response; fight back
manning 209 operating
unblemished 209 perfect; w/out any dirt or defects
expanse 209 wide stretch; breadth

no-man's-land 210 disputed ground in a battle, not yet held securely by either side
front line 210 closest position to their enemy that a military holds
leech 210 typo for *leach*, drain away
banned 211 forbid the singing of
petition 211 submit a formal, written request
wattage 212 measure of electrical power
inkling 213 suspicion; hint
fortified 214 defended
amplifies 214 makes louder
wretched 215 miserable and terribly unhappy
reconciliation 217 restoring of mutual understanding

Journal and Discussion Questions

1. List the points in the argument that are made by the brains, the soldiers, and the Mockingjay.
2. What meaning do you take from Gale's prediction about Coin? Is he correct? Explain.
3. After reading this chapter, do you think Gale is still a viable romantic partner for Katniss? Explain why you think as you do.
4. How does Katniss's past come to the fore in this chapter.
5. In recounting backstory, Katniss reflects at one point that she "should have known there was a problem right then." What does she mean?
6. Explain Haymitch's report on Peeta's progress.
7. Who do you think shot Katniss?
8. Why do you think Collins chose to have Katniss witness her own shooting on television?
9. Summarize the chapter from Gale's point of view.

Summary

Beetee, Lyme, Katniss, and Boggs respond to Gale's suggestion to blow up the Nut, and his answers are angry and insulting. Boggs suggests a modification of trapping and flushing out that involves leaving the train tunnel open. Beetee says that Coin needs to review the plan, and she approves it. Katniss, armed with her bow and dressed as the Mockingjay, and connected to Haymitch in 13 by earpiece, waits on the roof of the Justice Building in case there's a propo opportunity. The hoverplanes bomb the moutain and do not attract attention and antiaircraft fire until too late: the mountain is already collapsing. Katniss imagines what it's like inside, and recalls the day of her father's death, leading her to, again, question Gale's strategy. Haymitch orders Katniss inside in case of an airstrike. She recalls her last visit to this building on the Victory Tour, and the deaths of Clove and Cato. She talks with Boggs, who tries to assure her that they are taking a moderate approach and brings her a blanket. In the interim, Haymitch tells her that Peeta has, for the first time, heard a memory about someone connected to Katniss (her father) without losing his grip on reality. Katniss sees Gale go by with rebels ready for battle, and wishes for "the old" Peeta to put words to her feeling that shooting people who are trying to escape the mountain is wrong, but then questions her own views.

Cressida brings Katniss a microphone, as Haymitch tells her they want her to make a speech, which she reluctantly agrees to. He coaches her as she announces her presence, while two trains pull into the square from within the mountain. She ends up face to face with an armed escapee, ordering the rebels to hold their fire. He points his gun at her head. She speaks to him, and everyone, dropping her bow and saying she won't kill for the Capitol anymore, that she won't be their slave. She points out that the Capitol, not the people in the square, are the enemy, and asks the refugees from the Nut to join the rebellion. And then watches herself get shot on television.

Strategy 7

Analyzing Persuasive Techniques

Directions:
First, read the
information. Then,
answer the question
or questions.

Persuasive discourse attempts to change an audience's thoughts, feelings, beliefs, or values, or move the audience to action. A key part of Chapter 15 is Gale's attempts to persuade others to accept his strategy for the Nut and Katniss's (and Haymitch's) attempts to convince those who escaped the Nut to join the rebellion. We can analyze persuasive passages to see which techniques are being employed by each character.

Writers and speakers use a variety of techniques to make their communications persuasive. Some of these techniques are logical, reasonable, and accepted in our culture. Here are some examples of valuable techniques for persuasion:

- **Be courteous and control your tone of voice.** This keeps the focus on the point of contention.
- **Put the issue in perspective by referring to the big picture**.
- **Appeal to reason.** If something makes good sense, that in itself can be convincing.
- **Employ choice analysis** to understand people's freedom, responsbility, and culpability.
- **Suggest a compromise position** that recognizes the valid points of differing positions.
- **Appeal to authority.** Substantiate your claims by reminding or making others aware of the authority for your position.
- **Put yourself in others' shoes**.
- **Appeal to a principle, belief, or ideal that you and your audience share.** Finding common ground is helpful in persuading others.
- **Make reference to relevant protocol, rules, or laws.**
- **If you suspect there's confusion, clarify your position or ask a clarifying question.**
- **Make important distinctions.** Avoid grouping things that deserve separate consideration.

Other techniques that appeal to the audience's prejudices or to instincts that most people would consider base (like greed) are sometimes used, but are often seen as inappropriate. Also not appropriate are logical fallacies.

- **Appealing to the audience's emotions** may or may not be considered acceptable depending on the context and exactly what you say.
- **Name calling,** which attacks an opponent's character, is never considered appropriate. Both techniques are known as arguments **ad hominem—** appeals to the emotions or feelings rather than to the intellect.
- **Overgeneralizing** by drawing a wider conclusion that is supported by the evidence.
- **Making a false analogy**, by concluding from a superficial resemblance that conclusions that apply to one case can be transferred to another.
- **Assuming guilt by association**, condemning people based on the behavior or actions of their associates.

1. Analyze the persuasive techniques used by each of the following people in the argument about Gale's idea:

   a Gale   b. Katniss   c. Beetee   d. Boggs   e. Lyme

2. Analyze the persuasive techniques in the speech Katniss gives with Haymitch's support.

Chapter 16

Vocabulary

rustily 219 w/ difficulty
drip 219 measured method of drug delivery
socket 219 port into which tubes carrying medicine are plugged
rabbit warren 220 network of connected underground passages (figurative)
unbearable 221 deeply annoying
running rampant 222 spreading wildly
populace 223 people who live in a place
vetoes 224 refuses to allow
smash hit 226 something very successful
virtual impossibility 226 unimaginable

footwork 227 ability to execute dance steps
whatnot 228 so on
razzle-dazzle 229 showy display
wary 229 cautious
reproach 229 blame and disapproval
furtive 230 secretive, while attempting to avoid notice
remotely 230 the slightest bit
piece of work 232 messed up person; someone w/ a lot of problems
manipulative 232 cunning and controlling

Journal and Discussion Questions

1. Collins has given each book in the trilogy some lighter material. Identify these lighter sections for each book of the trilogy and discuss their function.

2. What is the plot justification for an elaborate wedding in the midst of a revolution?

3. Describe the current relationship between Katniss and Johanna.

4. Dancing has been mentioned more in connection with Capitol citizens—who dance in the streets of the Capitol.(*HG* p. 141) and whose dances Effie taught Katniss and Peeta prior the the Victory Tour (*CF* 79–80)—than in connection with District 12, about which Katniss says, "we know only a few dances at home, the kind that go with fiddle and flute music and require a good deal of space (*CF* p. 79). Given how carefully Collins set up the Chekhov's guns of Delly, Finnick being paid in secrets, and Peeta's promise to stay with Katniss "always," do you think a clearer reference to the love of dancing as a defining character of District 12 residents would have improved the flow for the audience? Explain.

5. Explain the meaning of *Panem et Circenses* in relationship to the Capitol's fragility and the differences between the Capitol and District 13.

6. Gale tells Katniss that the two of them know how to disagree. Do you think this ability is sufficient for them to maintain the closeness they once had? Explain.

7. Why is Katniss dancing with Prim significant?

8. Katniss says she wrote Peeta off in District 2. What earlier incident does this parallel?

9. Why is the framing of this chapter with the dream and conversation ironic?

10. Summarize the chapter from Peeta's point of view.

Summary

Katniss awakens in the hospital, dreaming of Peeta's promise to stay with her "always," and finds her ribs bandaged. She recalls that she was shot by someone hidden in the crowd. Johanna pulls back the hospital curtain and steals some of Katniss's morphling drip, and tells her she's lost her spleen. Johanna admits that she both hates and is jealous of Katniss. Johanna leaves as Gale enters, and Gale and Katniss argue about the acceptability of the action in 2. Katniss thinks it's a slippery slope; Gale disagrees, but points out that they know how to disagree and that 2 is in rebel hands, due to the Nut workers turning on the Capitol soldiers. A propo filmed in the hospital shows Katniss alive and threatening to enter the Capitol. One day, Plutarch comes by and explains how the Capitol differs from 13 and the role of *Panem et Circenses* in Capitol life. He plans to exploit this with a wedding propo featuring Finnick and Annie, which becomes a community affair. Katniss takes Annie to 12 to choose a Victory Tour dress, and the ceremony, with 300 guests, is led by Dalton from 10. Katniss is genuinely happy for the couple. Johanna urges her to let Snow see her dancing, and Katniss dances with Prim. Plutarch surprises everyone with a cake decorated by Peeta. As it's being served, Haymitch takes her aside and tells her Peeta wants to speak with her. She goes, and he sizes her up, accurately, but not nicely. She turns to leave, and he says he remembers about the bread. But then he asks if she loved him, and the conversation goes downhill. She walks out, hating him for now seeing her as, she thinks, she really is.

Strategy 8 — Analyzing a Dystopia

Strategy 8

Directions: First, read the information. Then, answer the question or questions.

The word *utopia* means "no place" in Greek, and was coined by Sir Thomas More in his 1516 book of that name which showed a perfect society on an imaginary island. Utopias—literary and in real life—are attempts to formulate ideal societies that deliver us from the social, political, and economic turmoil we experience. All real-world attempts have failed in one way or another.

Some writers have satirized the utopia, in a genre called *antiutopia* or *dystopia* (from the Greek meaning "bad or impaired place"). British philosopher John Stuart Mill coined the word *dystopia* in 1868 in a speech criticizing the British policy in Ireland. Literary dystopias show dehumanized rather than ideal societies, but like utopias, they critique contemporary problems. Dystopias tend to have certain characteristics, so when you read a book you suspect to be a dystopia, you can check to see if it has them.

Timeframe: Dystopias are generally set in the semi-distant to distant future.

Politics: Typically, a totalitarian, brutal government rules over a divided society, with a class of privileged citizens (which may only include those in the government, or a wider population), and a class of virtual (if not actual) slaves who serve the privileged.

Family Life: One way or another, family life is disrupted, by death at the hands of the state, separation, family members spying or reporting on each other, etc.

Religion: Religion is often suppressed, non-existent, or run by the ruling regime.

Identity: Conformity in one or more ways is usually required: attire, work, number of children allowed in a family, whom one marries, and other matters that are left to personal choice in a free society may be controlled.

Language: Euphemism is often used to both reshape perceptions of aberrations as normal and to justify indefensible practices.

Violence: Violence is used both to suppress non-conformity and by rebellious citizens attempting to overthrow the unjust government.

Nature: Nature may be alien or deadly, or citizens may be prevented from enjoying it.

History: The story of how the current state came to be is usually an important element of the dystopian story.

Protagonist: The protagonist may come from the oppressed classes or from within the government, having, for some reason, questioned it.

Outcome: Dystopias differ in portraying successful overthrows, protagomists who end up conforming, or indeterminate endings.

1. Do you think it is justifiable to classify the Hunger Games trilogy as a dystopia? Why or why not?

2. Do you think that Collins is criticizing our society? If so, which evils or ills of contemporary society do you think Collins is addressing? If not, what do you think her purpose is?

3. Do you think that the trilogy is a call to social action? If so, how? If not, why not?

Vocabulary

blindsided 233 hit by a completely unexpected attack

intervention 234 stepping in and attempting to alter a situation

unauthorized 234 done w/out official permission

disheveled 234 messy; untidy

vendetta 234 ongoing, bitter feud

negligence 235 failure to do what one should have done

accelerated 235 sped up

motivational 235 inspiring

gritting ... teeth 236 clamp one's teeth together to help keep one's resolve

keepsakes 239 small gifts that serve as reminders of the givers

incarnations 240 ways of acting

radiates 240 gives off

self-effacing 240 downplaying his own importance

easygoing 240 relaxed

estimation 240 evaluation of her value

goes off on a ... tear 240 launches into an attack (non-standard meaning)

perceptions 240 understandings; ideas

sugarcoating 240 making something look better than it actually is

adjoining 241 sharing a wall

censor 241 consider effects and appropriateness to decide whether or not to speak

rise to the bait 243 respond to remarks that are intended to provoke,

misusing 243 taking advantage of and deceiving

splay 243 spread

riveted 244 paying full attention

grime 245 dirt

Journal and Discussion Questions

1. There are multiple reasons why Katniss is not slated to go to the Capitol to fight. List them.
2. Do you think Coin's response to Katniss is fair? Explain.
3. What changes between Katniss and Johanna and why?
4. Why do you think Collins chose to not have the doctors offer Katniss the alternative treatment so that she had to find out from her trainer?
5. Analyze Katniss's use of the word *sugarcoating* to describe how Delly describes her to Peeta.
6. What do you make of Peeta's various comments at lunch?
7. What progress do Johanna and Katniss make towards getting to the Capitol?
8. Why do you think Collins gave Gale such a limited response to Katniss's suggestion that Peeta now sees her as she is?
9 Summarize the chapter from Johanna's point of view.

Summary

Katniss is blindsided by Haymitch's news that she is not going to the Capitol. Racing to Command, she confronts Coin, arguing that being the Mockingjay means she must go. Coin counters that the role of the Mockingjay was to unify the districts, a task now completed: she'll be flown in for the surrender. When Katniss says that Gale is going, Coin counters that Gale has been training; Katniss has not. Boggs acknowledges her capabilities, but points out that she's not a soldier. After more argument, Katniss says she has to go because the Capitol destroyed her district, and Coin consents to a possible review of her case if she starts training immediately. Since Johanna is in the same situation, they create an alliance. Also, their trainer tells Katniss of an alternate treatment to heal her ribs quicker, and Katniss accepts, though its extremely painful, and she can't have painkillers, cutting off Johanna's supply as well. After a rough night, the pair gets through the day of training and move into a compartment together, where Katniss allows Johanna to look through her special possessions.

One day after praise from their trainer, they head to the dining hall, where there is a meal of real beef stew. They sit with Delly, Annie, Finnick, and Gale. Partway through the meal, Katniss realizes that Peeta, handcuffed and accompanied by two guards, is asking to join them, and sits by Johanna. Although he speaks kindly to Annie, he makes offensive remarks to Finnick and Katniss, angering Gale, who leaves with Katniss. When Katniss says maybe Peeta sees her as she is, Gale denies it. Johanna comes later and reports that Delly lost her temper with Peeta. Recalling Johanna's dinner remark about having an adjoining cell to Peeta's and hearing him scream, Katniss has nightmares.

Chapter 18

The Star Squad; Peeta Joins the Star Squad

Vocabulary

with a vengeance 246 w/ enthusiasm

be a contender 246 have a chance to win

simulated 246 made in imitation of something else

jams 246 sticks in such a way that it no longer works

sniper 246 marksman specializing in long shots from a concealed position

manacles 247 handcuffs; shackles

spat 247 argument about something minor

proficiency 248 skill; capability

backlog 248 pile up; accumulation

brute force 248 strength in contrast to finesse or thought

nail … to the wall 248 punish severely

overthinking 248 thinking so much about something, that one becomes uncertain

soldierly 250 like a soldier, i.e., disciplined and obedient

sharpshooters 250 people particularly skilled in shooting; marksmen

holographic image 250 3-D image formed by interfering w/ light beams

pod 250 container holding some deadly device or other

absconded with 251 stole

cockily 251 impudently; in a smart-alecky way

ferret out 253 search for w/ dogged determination

flashback 253 sudden, vivid recollection of a past event, often a trauma

regulation 254 required

anonymous 254 not able to be identified by unique characteristics

abrasive 254 harsh; showing no concern for others

compelling 255 convincing

militarized 256 equipped with features suitable for war

farsighted 256 having greater abilities with distance vision than near vision

compliant 257 cooperative; agreeable

makeshift 258 set up to serve immediate need, but not complete or well-made

encampment 265 city of tents for soldiers

pitch 259 erect a tent

deserting 259 abandoning their duty

disinformation 259 false information used in a military campaign to mislead the enemy

if looks could kill 260 idiom meaning, "he glared at me angrily"

foot soldier 260 soldier who fights on foot rather than from horseback, an armored vehicle, or an aircraft

outwardly 260 publicly

intersection 260 meeting place of two or more streets

remedial 260 intended for students who need extra review to grasp the concept

glorified 260 wonderful example of, full of stunning features

squadron 260 fighting unit composed of a specific group of soldiers

Journal and Discussion Questions

1. What suggestion does Plutarch make in this chapter that Katniss rejects out of hand. What does it show about his character? Cite other evidence to support your view of Plutarch.

2. What insight does Katniss have into how others perceive her?

3. What is Katniss's first impression of the Star Squad. How does it change by the end of the chapter?

4. Although Katniss and Finnick perceive that entering the Capitol will be undertaking another round of the Games, they also see some differences. What similarities and differences do you see, including the ones they point out?

5. What has led to the end of the war being played out as a street fight without air involvement?,

6. At one point, Katniss surmises that those in charge don't want to lose the Mockingjay, but at the same time, want to change her role to foot soldier. Do you agree that her surmise seems correct when she makes it? Explain.

7. Explain the workings of the Holo in your own words.

8. What do you think of Plutarch's response to Leeg 2's death?

9. Analyze Katniss's analysis of Peeta's arrival. What evidence is there that Katniss's conclusion is correct? What is against it? What effects do you expect Peeta's presence to have?

10. Summarize this chapter by drawing a map showing all the locations mentioned in it. Feel free to make up what you can't establish from the book (e.g., relative size and distance).

Summary

After the encounter with Peeta and learning more about his and Johanna's torture, Katniss ups the intensity of her investment in training, and being placed, along with Johanna, in an additional class in Simulated Street Combat increases her hopes that she may get to go to the Capitol and fight. In the Block (as they call it), they simulate missions in which everything goes wrong.

New propos showing the victors training with the rebels are underway when Katniss sees Peeta at their training, still guarded, but with manacles off, and learning how to assemble a gun. Plutarch assures her that it's "all for the camera," so that they can satisfy everyone in Panem's curiosity about Peeta, and establish that he's fighting for the rebels. He suggests photos of Katniss and Peeta together, and Katniss walks away without responding.

A few days before the invasion is to begin, their trainer tells Katniss and Johanna that she's recommended that they take the combat-ready exam—which consists of an obstacle course, a written exam on tactics, a weapons proficiency test, and a simulated combat situation on the block, and they are to report to the first part immediately. The first three go well, but there's a hold-up at the Block, during which they learn that this test is designed to target each potential soldier's weaknesses. Katniss conceives of a number of weaknesses that they might target in her, including minimal training, limited physical force, and standing out too much.

Johanna goes first, then Katniss. Katniss's situation appears too easy until she sees a gasoline drum that she sees needs to be blown up, and at first she thinks that's the key test. Then, her squadron leader tells her to hit the ground, and—realizing that not taking orders is clearly what the military will perceive as her biggest weakness—she fights off her desire to be the one to blow-up the gasoline, and does as she's told, earning her an assignment to invasion squad 451, though oddly, she is told to report to Command rather than to the barber for the regulation hair cut. Boggs greets her in Command, and tells her that she's assigned to his special unit of sharpshooters, which includes Gale and Finnick, leading Katniss to think their mission must be important.

Plutarch gives a presentation on their mission, showng a holographic image of a block of the Capitol and revealing the existence of "pods"—deadly obstacles created at various times since the Dark Days. The Capitol does not realize that the rebels escaped with information about their locations. Katniss and Finnick move toward the display. Finnick begins the announcement of the Seventy-sixth Hunger Games, and Katniss finishes it, and then they both act to deflect the conclusion that they think will be drawn from the Capitol's similarity to the arena.

When they are dismissed, Finnick and Katniss meet in the hallway and discuss what to tell their loved ones, and Katniss points out a significant difference between this and earlier Hunger Games: Snow is a player now. Their conversation is interrupted by Haymitch, who tells them that Johanna is in the hospital, having failed the simulation due to her aversion to water after being electrocuted as part of the Capitol torture. Finnick goes to her, but Katniss gains Boggs's permission to go outside so she can make Johanna a pine needle cachet—both to remind her of her home in District 7, and to give her a possession, since she has none. When she delivers it, Johanna makes Katniss swear on the lives of her family that she will kill Snow.

In the several remaining days of training before shipping out, Katniss, Gale, and Finnick practice together with the weapons Beetee made for them, and they get to know the other members of their squad a bit better: Jackson, Boggs's second in command, Leeg 1 and Leeg 2, and Mitchell and Homes, all excellent shots. Then one morning, Plutarch joins them and announces that they have been chosen for a special mission—not to assassinate Snow, as Katniss hopes, but to be the Star Squad, the on-screen "face of the invasion." The squad is shocked, disappointed, and defiant, although Katniss is noticeably silent, until she perceives that being too quiet will be suspicious and voices a mild challenge.

Katniss both equivocates with and conceals information from her mother and sister, but says, honestly, that she feels better knowing the Prim is somewhere Snow can't touch her. Prim says that they'll be free of Snow the next time they meet, and Katniss—taking the pearl that Peeta gave her as a "token of the boy with the bread," heads for the train that will take her to one of the mountain tunnels that leads to the Capitol. After making the six-hour trek to the base camp, near the train station where tributes arrive, the squad learns that advance into the city depends on sweeping the pod-infested streets ahead of them and that air power will not be a factor in this phase of the war. For the next three days, they shoot targeted pods, and lots of other things so the Capitol won't know they have intelligence on the pods, and Gale, Finnick, and Katniss are never chosen for special missions. They complain somewhat, but Katniss pursues her own agenda, studying her paper map and wishing for a Holo. On the fourth morning, Leeg 2 is killed when taking out a mislabelled pod. Plutarch promises a speedy replacement, and the following evening, Peeta arrives, sent—he says—by the specific order of Coin. Katniss takes this to mean that Coin thinks Katniss is more use dead than alive.

Vocabulary

Look at each group of words. Tell why it is important in the story.

1. sharpshooters, soldierly, holographic image
2. setback, downgraded
3. foot soldier, deserting, disinformation
4. power plays, back-stabbing, blackmail, arson
5. smash hit, virtual impossibility, razzle-dazzle
6. knockout gas, power failure, detonation, disruption
7. cold collar, chafes, spinal cord, airway, larynx
8. quarry, stonecutters, hangar, fortress
9. shellfish, viruses, aorta, antidotes
10. sugarcoating, censor, rise to the bait, splay
11. cell disintegrators, drones, biological weapons
12. cavern, hewn, dank, brownouts

Essay Topics

1. In Chapter 11, Boggs says that September starts the following week, and Katniss figures that Snow has therefore had Peeta for 5–6 weeks. Work out the timing of the book so far based on this and explain how you reached your conclusions.

2. Do you think Haymitch already knew when he was comforting Katniss in Chapter 11 what District 13's next move would be? Provide evidence to support your answer.

3. Collins uses the word *irretrievable* to describe the jabberjay version of Prim (*CF* p. 340) and Peeta's condition after being hijacked (*MJ*, Chapter 13, p. 191). What meaning do you find in the repetition?

4. What effect, if any, do you think that the length of time since Snow has appeared in the action has on your investment or interest in Katniss killing him? Explain your response.

5. Do you think Katniss's insight into how others would perceive her greatest weakness is in keeping with her character as Collins has developed it? Explain, citing evidence to support your position.

6. What earlier incidents does Finnick's and Katniss's split announcement of the Seventy-sixth Hunger Games parallel? What conclusions do you draw from this? Why do they engage in damage control afterwards?

7. How is the "Seventy-sixth Hunger Games" similar to and different from the Seventy-fourth and Seventy-fifth?

8. What is ironic about the Capitol being filled with pods like the arenas?

9. Compare and contrast Katniss's arrival in the Capitol in all three books.

10. Having completed Part II "The Assault" what do you understand the title to mean?

11. What is the reversal in Act II of *Mockingjay*?

12. If you were the author of this story, what would happen next? How would you develop the plot?

13. If Katniss is right about Coin's intent in sending Peeta to join the Star Squad, what else follows?

14. Compare and contrast Peeta's presence in the Star Squad to his presence in the Career Group in *HG*.

15. What steps do you think an "angry, independently thinking victor" (*MJ*, p. 251) will do in the situation Katniss is in at the close of Part II?

16. Given what you know at this point, how do you understand the title of Part III: "The Assassin"?

Chapter 19

PART III: "THE ASSASSIN" "Real or Not Real"; Boggs Steps on a Mine

Vocabulary

dilemma 267 difficult choice between equally undesirable alternatives
broken down 269 being hit by previously unfelt emotions
fixation 269 consuming, obsessive interest
stranded 269 abandoned without hope of return
grossly 270 completely
revisit 270 bring back to mind and reconsider
cessation 270 end
double-knot 271 knot twice
uninspiring 273 not stirring the feelings as an effective call to action

playact 273 pretend to fight
execution 273 a death sentence
captors 273 those capturing an enemy soldier or soldiers
residential 273 filled with homes (rather than businesss or industry)
worrisome 273 causing concern
voltage 274 electrical potential
abduct 274 kidnap
grisly 275 horrifying
hazy 275 covered w/ air that is clouded by smoke or particles
alcove 276 recess in a wall

Journal and Discussion Questions

1. What new understanding of Coin did you gain from this chapter?
2. Katniss is not grateful to Boggs, because she feels in his debt, making it harder for her to determine to steal his Holo and desert. What parallels do you see?
3. Why does Haymitch confront Katniss in their phone call?
4. What explanation does Katniss offer for ignoring the problem of rescuing Peeta? Do you accept her rationale? Explain why you think as you do.
5. What does Peeta say that might be a clue to helping him recover?
6. What clues does Collins give that the Star Squad operation in this chapter won't be routine?
7. Sumarize this chapter from Peeta's point of view.

Summary

Angered by Peeta's arrival, Boggs orders Jackson to set up a 24-hour, two-person guard, and takes Katniss on a walk away from the tents. Katniss points out that the extent of bad memories in the Capitol means Peeta will try to kill her despite the guard, but Boggs promises to keep him in line. Katniss asks why Coin wants her dead, and after saying that Coin does not admit to this, he tells Katniss that Coin never liked her, wanted to rescue Peeta rather than Katniss, but couldn't get agreement, and was further angered by Katniss's demand for victor immunity. Katniss's fine performance as the Mockingjay would have laid it to rest except that Coin wants to be leader of the new regime, and she's clear that Katniss is not going to support her wholeheartedly, so there's only one thing left that Katniss can contribute to the rebel cause / Coin's political ascension: become a martyr. Boggs promises again to protect her, and Katniss is frustrated because she feels in his debt, so, guilty about her plans to steal his Holo and decamp.

Katniss, with Boggs's blessing, joins the rotation to watch Peeta. Gale asks her if she wants him to kill Peeta, but—rattled by his brutality—she declines. Gale reveals that he knows her plans, and she agrees that when she leaves, he can come along. In a phone call with Haymitch, he upbraids her for blaming Peeta for what he can't help and abandoing him in a way Peeta never would have done to her. He reminds her of their deal to try to save him. Katniss accepts that she should help Peeta, but can't get started. She does, however, find the grace to answer his first comment to her, which she finds unfair, by saying that she always considered him an ally. Peeta voices his problem: that he can't tell what's real, and Finnick says that he should ask, like Annie does. He first asks about Katniss's favorite color, and she confirms his recollection and tells him his, and some other of his characteristics. It becomes a game, in which the squad support him.

The squad receives notice of a complicated propo. On the way, Peeta recognizes Pollux as an Avox, and recollects the deaths of Darius and Lavinia, causing Katniss to seek comfort with Gale. Everyone gets in place, and the propo begins. Gale is assigned the real target. As Cressida has them repeat their moves to take close-ups, Mitchell hams up to show desperation, and Boggs reprimands the laughter that results. Shifting to position his Holo, Boggs steps backwards onto an orange paving stone, and a bomb detonates, blowing off his legs.

Writer's Forum 4

Analyzing Nuance in Word Meanings

Directions:
First, read the information. Then, answer the question or questions.

Synonyms are sometimes defined as words that mean the same thing. This is not quite true. No two words mean exactly the same thing. Even if the denotation—the dictionary definition—is the same for two words, the connotation—the emotional associations and "flavor" the two words have—is always different. Shades of meaning refers to the differences found in words that are synonyms.

Some things that affect how we view a word are:

- familiarity or lack of familiarity
- sound
- length
- famous occurrences
- formality/informality
- context
- range of meanings (denotations)
- emotional overtones (connotations)
- etymology
- previous use by the person using it

There are other possibilities as well.

1. Use the list of word characteristics above to annotate the list of words (reproduced below) that Peeta says he uses to try to figure out Katniss:

Friend

Lover

Victor

Enemy

Fiancée

Target

Mutt

Neighbor

Hunter

Tribute

Ally

Chapter 20

Katniss Assumes Command; Peeta Asks for Death

Vocabulary

security clearance 278 status granted in degrees as one rises in an organization, and allowed access to secret information

geyser 278 hot spring that erupts in a column of water and steam

minesweeping 279 clearing mines from an area

electromagnetic pulse device 281 device that uses electromagnetic energy to interrupt the signals of and damage electronic equipment

homicidal rage 281 violent anger combined w/ plans to commit murder

plausible 282 believable

unsustainable 282 not able to be kept at the current level

self-appointed 283 chosen w/ no orders or support from those in charge

corrosive 284 able to eat away materials by chemical action

succumb to 285 be overcome by

dismantled 286 taken apart; rendered harmless

peter out 286 fade; ebb

jimmies 286 forces open

evacuating 286 hastily leaving a dangerous place to seek safety

delusional 287 characterized by believing in things that are untrue

complexity 287 state of being complicated

revel 288 feel great pleasure in response to something

Journal and Discussion Questions

1. Recount and explain Boggs's comments to Katniss in this chapter.
2. What does each squad member do after Boggs falls until they get inside?
3. What do Peeta's first sentences upon regaining consciousness reveal about him?
4. Why isn't the squad in touch with the invading encampment?
5. Analyze the persuasive techniques that convince the squad to follow Katniss.
6. How does the emergency broadcast help the squad? Whom is it likely to hurt?
7. Summarize the chapter by distinguishing events that help/hurt Katniss's plan.

Summary

There's a second explosion. Homes tries to treat Boggs, who orders Katniss to find the Holo, while Finnick attempts to revive Messalla, and Jackson is trying to reach the camp on a field communicator. Katniss is prepared to comfort Boggs as he dies, but he's busy with the Holo, and then uses it to transfer "prime security clearance" to Katniss. Jackson orders a retreat, as Finnick directs attention down the street, where a black, oily spout is creating a wave, heading their way. Gale and Leeg 1 attempt a minesweep, clearing at least one bomb, and Homes and Katniss drag Boggs after them. Suddenly Katniss is yanked backward, and sees Peeta preparing to bring his rifle down on her head in time to roll away. Mitchell tackles him, but Peeta uses his feet to push Mitchell off, where he lands on a pod that traps him in a net filled with barbed wire. Gale and Leeg 1 shoot off the locks on a building and then try to shoot through the cables that hold the net to get Mitchell down, while others restrain Peeta. Homes and Katniss get Boggs into the appartment. Castor and Pollux carry in Peeta, whom Jackson handcuffs, and they lock in in a closet. Finnick carries Messalla in, Leeg 1, Cressida, and Gale join them. Boggs puts the Holo in Katniss's hands and says, "Don't trust them. Don't go back. Kill Peeta. Do what you came to do." Then he dies.

Finnick points out that there must be surveillance tapes of them, and Castor agrees, surmising that they set of the black wave in response to seeing the squad. Jackson notes that an electromagnetic pulse was likely responsible for making their communicators go dead, but says she can get them back to camp, and reaches for the Holo, which Katniss refuses to give her, telling Jackson that Boggs assigned it to Katniss, which Jackson doesn't believe, even when Homes backs Katniss up. To persuade the squad, Katniss claims to be on a special mission for President Coin to kill Snow before the population becomes unsustainable, and only Boggs knew. Jackson doesn't believe her until Cressida backs Katniss up saying Plutarch wanted Snow's assassination televised and also volunteers that Peeta's presence is to help them navigate Snow's mansion, where his interviews were filmed.

Katniss leads them out, and offers everyone a chance to return to camp, but no one does. They enter an apartment five blocks away, and hear explosions. A television comes to life on its own, and they learn that they have been identified cond pronounced dead. Gale asks about their next move, and Peeta says it's obviously to kill him (Peeta).

Chapter 21

Two Farewells to Katniss; Underground

Vocabulary

conflicted 290 exhibiting internal conflict
reliability 291 trustworthiness
simplify 291 make easier
divvy up 293 divide equally
output 293 work done
inept 293 clumsy
aroma 293 pleasant smell
masterful 294 skillful; extremely well done
demoralized 294 w/out hope or confidence
rabble 294 ordinary people (the term reflects a sense of superiority to such people)
antics 294 outrageous behavior
eulogy 294 speech of praise for the dead
freedom fighter 294 person who uses acts of war to overthrow an unjust government
oppressors 294 those who unjustly exercise of authority to mistreat citizens
grace period 295 extra time free from consequences
comforter 295 warm blanket made of a shell and filling
down 295 goose feathers
coordinates 295 numbers that indicate location points
moot point 296 irrelevan
interlaced 296 mixed together
maintenance 296 used to access and fix building systems
on contact 296 when touched

budge 296 move even the smallest amount
disclose 297 reveal
voluntarily 297 of one's own free will
bulky 298 large and inconveniently shaped
break into 298 enter using force and w/out permission
utility 298 publicly provided services: electricity, water, gas, and sewage
treads 298 strips of material designed to help one keep one's footing
bowels 298 parts deep underround
sewage 298 waste carried in water from sinks and toilets into sewers
dispirited 299 lacking hope and enthusiasm
minefield 299 region covered with concealed land mines
drainage 299 for directing water away
offshoots 300 branches
obscure 300 hidden
alertness 300 being awake and aware
input 301 enter data into a computer
untangle 301 put into order
chugging back 301 swallowing continuously w/out pausing or chewing
fluorescent 302 alternate to incandescent
unresisting 302 w/out argument
exhalations 303 releases of breath**

Journal and Discussion Questions

1. Identify persuasive techniques used in the debate about Peeta's death request?
2. Explain how Katniss's recollection of "The Hanging Tree" is apt or why it isn't.
3. Which actions in this chapter show change in Peeta? In Katniss? Explain.
4. Compare and contrast the two televised farewells to Katniss.
5. Summarize the chapter by identifying how challenges to the mission were surmounted.

Summary

Peeta argues for the squad killing him. After an internal struggle, Katniss tells Peeta that he's needed for the mission, and directs the squad to search for food. Peeta gives Katniss a can of the lamb stew that was her favorite Capitol meal and formed the special meal in the cave in *HG* (p. 302). While they are eating, the television lights up and images of the (presumed) dead (Boggs, Gale, Finnick, Peeta, Katniss) are shown, as in the arena. Snow is shown congratulating the Peacekeepers for ridding Panem of the Mockingjay, which he predicts will demoralize the rebels and turn the tide of the war. He characterizes Katniss as a person of no skill or talent, but important to the rebels who have no real leadership. His speech is interrupted by President Coin, presenting herself as the leader of the rebellion and praising Katniss, holding her up as a beacon of strength for rebels who need inspiration to "rid Panem of its oppressors," followed by a poster photo of Katniss. Regaining control, Snow promises that the following day, when they recover Katniss's body, they will have reality: "a dead girl who could save no one, not even herself." The team chooses to go underground to stay ahead of the Peacekeeprs, using the maintenance shaft, bringing a reluctant Peeta. Pollux is upset because he was forced to work underground after he became an Avox, but as Peeta points out, he becomes the squads biggest asset, leading them away from the apartment and finding a resting spot. Katniss gets Peeta to elucidate his comment about shininess, and smooths his hair, the first time she has voluntarily touched him. He realizes that she is trying to protect him. As they prepare to move on, they hear a repeated hiss of "*Katniss.*"

Chapter 22

Vocabulary

trophies 304 evidence of other killings
eject 305 force out
blank cartridge 305 a cartridge that has no bullet, so it fires without harming anyone
monstrosities 306 monstrous and malformed, twisted genetic experiments
discretion 306 avoiding revealing their location and plans
congestion 308 overcrowding; traffic jams
flipping out 308 losing self-control; becoming extremely agitated
reptilian 309 like those of reptiles
decapitated (are) 309 have their heads bitten off
skitter 309 move rapidly and w/out heavy footfalls

runoff 310 drained material
vapor 310 smoke and/or vapors condensed in clouds
slithering 310 moving this way and that, w/ bellies close to or on the ground,
lathered 311 filled with foam, indicating intense excitement
evocative 311 strong in bringing up memories
toxicity 311 extremely poisonous nature
psychological twist 311 feature aimed at destruction of the mind, rather than the body
grazed 312 scraped the skin, w/ little or no bleeding
normalcy 314 the normal, expected state of things

Journal and Discussion Questions

1. When else has Katniss aimed her bow at Peeta because she misunderstood him?
2. Katniss considers whether she has turned Peeta into a piece in her private games. Has she? Cite evidence to support your position.
3. List the surprises in this chapter. Why is each important?
4. Use the Choice Analysis Tool to analyze the squad members' choices in this chapter as deeply as you can, given the limitations of first-person narration.
5. Write an ending for *Mockingjay* in which you pick up after Chapter 22 ends on p. 314. Do not look ahead as you do this. (If you know what happens, write an alternate ending.) Keep in mind foreshadowing and important plot points.
6. Summarize the "grace periods" and other breaks in the action in the trilogy.

Summary

Katniss realizes their grace period is over, but is not sure if Peeta is part of the attack, until he shouts out a warning. Katniss suggests they split up, but the squad refuses, so she shifts the weapons around to arm the camera crew, but not Peeta. The mutts are at a distance, but the squad can't erase their scent, and Katniss expects the mutts will be faster than humans. Sticking to a plan to move towards Snow's mansion, they speed ahead, albeit more sloppily than usual. After three blocks, the begin to hear cries, which Peeta identifies as the screams of Avoxes, leading them to realize that the mutts will kill anyone in their path, not just Katniss, who again suggests that the squad split up, and is refused again. They hear the hissing from below now, too, which interrupts their planned path. As Katniss and Pollux seek an alternate route on the Holo, Katniss starts to gag due to the odor of roses and stumbles into the Transfer and leads the squad forward, shooting out pods as she goes. Focused on her plan for the "meat grinder" ahead, Finnick has to alert her to what has happened behind: Messalla caught by a pod. While the squad stands shocked transfixed, it is Peeta who urges them forward. At the next intersection, Katniss sees Peacekeepers heading towards them, and they fire at each other across the Meat Grinder pod, with the Star Squad living up to their name until the lizard mutts arrive, swarming over the Peacekeepers and ripping off their heads. Katniss leads the squad around the corner, activates the Meat Grinder to slow down the mutts, and asks Pollux to get them aboveground. As they cross a narrow bridge and start to head up a ladder, Katniss realizes that Jackson and Leeg 1 aren't with them. Homes tells her they stayed at the Grinder. Gale shoots out the far end of the bridge as the mutts reach it. Following Pollux up to the next level, Katniss looks back, seeing Finnick fighting three mutts before Gale forces her up. She detonates the Holo, Pollux locks the cover over the pipe through which they emerged, and Katniss sees that only Pollux, Gale (with a neck wound), Cressida, and Peeta remain with her. When they move to go, Peeta doesn't rise. He tells Katniss that he can't hold on, and she kisses him, saying "Don't let him take you from me . . . Stay with me." He answers, "Always." Arriving at street level, they find themselves in a utility room with a woman who recognizes Katniss. Katniss shoots her.

Strategy 9

Appreciating Genre Fusion

Directions: *First, read the information. Then, answer the question or questions.*

In addition to fitting many of the patterns of dystopia, the Hunger Games trilogy arguably fits descriptions for several other genres. As with dystopias, you can look for key elements of any genre you may suspect the author is including in the mix.

War Novels

Many war novels are historical fiction, though there are also sci fi war tales (e.g., *Star Wars*). War novels focus on descriptions of the battleground, weaponry, tactics, strategy, and key personnel, as well as the meaning of the conflict. There are often episodic battle descriptions and heroic action, as well as atrocities of war depicted, and the capture and treatment of prisoners may play a part.

Monster SciFi

Often connected with movies and special effects, monsters battling innocent humans and the choice analysis of monsters (e.g., Frankenstein's monster) who may be tools of an evil genius both form key themes in these tales, as is genetic engineering, and in some, there are battles between monsters. The monsters are often distinguished from humans by size and/or having features from the animal world or characteristics from multiple animals (e.g., Gill-man in *The Creature from the Black Lagoon*).

Thriller

Thrillers focus on the effects on the reader, relying on suspense and excitement, and employing cliffhangers, shockers, and frequently placing the protagonist(s) in treacherous situations. Fight scenes and chase scenes abound, and mind-games (psychological warfare) is often employed. The villain in a thriller often drives the plot, presenting obstacles that the protagonist(s) must overcome to stay alive (or kill the villain or both). In a thriller, there is often corruption, a lack of trust, and danger that is beyond what the main character realizes.

Action–Adventure

Action–adventure contains features of the action genre, which shows a protagonist who has to undertake exciting feats of physical prowess in order to reach his or her goal and the adventure genre, which also focuses on an inherently dangerous quest or undertaking, usually in exotic or un-usual locations.

Romance

Romances often take as a tenet that true love can conquer anything. It tends to feature young, attractive lovers, who fall in love after an initial period of dislike and are then separated by a misunderstanding or circum-stances, but eventually end up back together.

1. Write an essay teasing out the genres of the Hunger Games trilogy.

Chapter 23

Vocabulary

mantel 316 structure around a fireplace
determinedly 316 w/ very firm purpose
passerby 317 pedestrian passing the area
manicured 317 well-tended
poky 318 small and shabby
storefront 318 street-facing store entry
semi-feline 318 part cat (part human)
distrustfully 318 suspiciously; w/out trust
repellence 319 state of causing disgust
public eye 319 view of others
by extension 319 taking the argument one
   more step
sutures 321 stitches used in surgery to
   hold the edges of a wound together
mercy of (at the) 322 completely in the
   power of

all-consuming passion 322 complete and
   utter dedication
ditch 322 leave behind; escape from
forays 323 sudden trips into enemy
   territory (metaphorical)
retracing 323 going over mentally
tassels 323 decorative groups of threads,
   knotted on one end and free on the other
infiltrated 324 secretly gained entrance to
   an enemy base
embellishments 325 enhancements
vigilant 325 watchful
viable 327 believable
obliged 327 required mm
bounties 327 MM rewards

Journal and Discussion Questions

1. Peeta repeats several lines from earlier in the series in this chapter. Identify them and tell the import of the repetition.
2. What leads to the differences in Gale's and Katniss's views of the success—so far—of the mission to kill Snow?
3. Does the explanation of who believed what fit with the details in Chapter 20?
4. According to Katniss, why would Plutarch be thrilled with recent events?
5. Did the squad have good reason to believe Katniss could kill Snow? Explain.
6. Identify the parallel scene in which Katniss said only one voice could reach her. Whose voice was it? What does the change mean?
7. What do you think Gale means by, "Katniss will pick whoever she thinks she can't survive without"? Explain why you think as you do.
8. Predict Coin's reaction and actions when she learns Katniss is alive.
9. Summarize the chapter from Tigris's point of view.

Summary

There's no one else in the apartment, but—expecting to be found at any time—the squad must move on. In the homeowner's well-stocked closets, they find plenty of materials to disguise themselves. Grabbing food and first-aid supplies, they join the crowd of displaced citizens moving by. From the emergency report, they figure out that it's not yet known who died in the mutt attack. Cressida figures out a potential hideout, and leads them to a fur undergarment store five blocks from Snow's mansion, babbling about shopping as a cover. There they meet Tigris, a former stylist who had too much surgical enhancement. Cressida tells her that Plutarch said she could be trusted, which makes it possible she will then report them. When Tigris sees Katniss, she opens a secret panel to a basement hideout. As they enter, Katniss attempts to win her support by voicing her conclusion that Snow banned Tigris from the games and announcing that she is going to kill him. Settling into the basement, they make beds of pelts, treat Gale's wound, and sleep. Katniss dreams of a long search for home, accompanied by Effie Trinket.

Katniss awakens in late afternoon, eats, reviews the dead members of the squad, and decides she needs to confess her fabrication to what's left of the squad. She learns, then, that everyone knew she was lying from the start, and that making the opportunity to kill Snow a condition of becoming the Mockingjay made her intentions clear. Katniss says the mission has been a disaster, and Gale counters that they've breached the enemy base, created stunning propos, and created chaos in the attempts to locate them. Peeta points out that everyone in the squad believed that Katniss could kill Snow. But they are not able to come up with a good plan. They learn that Tigris has not contacted Plutarch as they eat food she has provided and watch the news. Back in the basement, they decide to split up, and Peeta and Gale discuss Katniss. Gale says she'll chooose whichever of them she thinks she can't survive without, and Peeta does not protest.

Chapter 24

The Squad Splits Up; Gale Is Captured; Prim Dies

Vocabulary

compatibility 330; being like-minded

sway me 330 convince me to change my mind

refute 330 declare to be false

exploited 330 taken advantage of

pâte 330 paste of minced ingredients

unmanned 331 w/out a human driver

spectacle 331 attention-grabbing sight

bounty on her head 332 reward for her capture or death

milling about 332 move around, but w/out definite purpose or goal

depleting 332 lessening; diminishing

cache 332 hidden supply

staged-looking 334 appearing to be scripted, not real and spontaneous

appropriated 334 taken by the government for use w/ or w/out payment

swell 334 grow larger

unpredictable 335 not able to be foreseen

diversion 335 distraction

fitful 336 disturbed; broken

surge through me 338 flood my memory

inquisitive 339 inclined to wonder about things and ask questions; curious;

mows down 339 kills w/ barrage of bullets

scuttle 339 run quickly w/ short steps, while trying to stay concealed

transfixed 340 absorbed by looking at

parboils 341 partially cooks by boiling

curlicues 341 corkscrews

backpedal 341 move quickly backwards mm

orifices 341 the body's natural openings

straddle 343 extend across

grating 343 crisscross structure of bars that allows airflow but prevents access

human shield 345 group of innocent people, strategically placed for protection from attack

Journal and Discussion Questions

1. Analyze Katniss's analysis of what Gale said about her..

2. In response to the news report of the beating of someone who is minimally similar to Peeta, Cressida says, "People have gone wild." How would you respond?

3. Katniss and Gale agree to leave Peeta behind. How does this square with Peeta being "necessary" to the mission (p. 292)?

4. What parallel do you find with the tactics employed in the parachute attack?

5. Which side killed Prim? Cite evidence to support your conclusions.

6. Summarize the chapter from Gale's point of view.

Summary

Katniss is offended by her interpretation of Gale's comments, and blames both Gale and Peeta. In the morning, she dismisses her feelings, as they eat and watch coverage of a new rebel strategy designed to pre-trigger pods, but which backfires when the Capitol deactivates and reactivates pods, catching the rebels by surprise. Then, civiliian evacuations are ordered, and the refugees can be seen passing the shop. Tigris goes out to spy, while Katniss ponders her situation should the rebels take the Capitol. Tigris returns and reports that citizens are seeking, and not finding, shelter for the night, and a broadcast announces mandatory hosting of the displaced, which—Peeta points out—could apply to Tigris and her shop, putting them at risk if they stay. A further report details the crowd murdering a young man who superficially looks like Peeta, so traveling with Peeta endangers the mission in a new way. Washing the dishes, Gale and Katniss decide to split off from the others. When Katniss announces the plan, Peeta responds that he'll go out and try to create a diversion, return to Tigris's if he feels he's losing control, and take the nightlock tablet that Gale offers him if he's about to be captured. After they sleep and eat, Tigris uses her stylist abilities on them, and they head out: Cressida and Pollux first, then Gale and Katniss, with Peeta slated to follow. Katniss hugs Peeta before leaving, evoking many memories. Alerted by a young girl's apparent interest in her, Katniss is warning Gale when rebels on the rooftops open fire. Hugging the wall, they keep moving, getting guns from a wounded and dead Peacekeeper. They avoid two pods that capture many and a group of passing Peacekeepers. The street breaks open, leaving Katniss dangling, but pulls herself out and locates Gale, clinging to a door grating. Katniss shoots the lock, and the door opens to reveal Peacekeepers who drag Gale in. Katniss misses his mouthing of "shoot me," but runs when he yells. Reaching Snow's mansion, she finds a human shield of children. A plane with Capitol insignia drops parachutes, as the rebels arrive. Twenty parachutes explode, and rebel medics run to help. Katniss spots Prim and calls out. As Prim turns to her and calls her name, the rest of the parachutes go off.

Chapter 25

Vocabulary

unquenchable 348 not able to be stopped from burning

adrift 348 w/out purpose; confused and lost

saturates 348 soaks

rawness 350 state of being red and painful

clinches it 350 is the deciding factor

emotional trauma 351 damage to one's sense of security and safety caused by a deeply disturbing experience

mopping up 351 destroying any remaining pockets of resistance

salvageable 352 able to be saved

patchwork quilt 352 bedspread of irregularly-shaped pieces of random fabrics

sentenced 353 assigned the punishment of

muted 353 (of color) not bright mm

sumptuous 354 beautiful and costly

pruned 354 trimmed to keep healthy

pruning shears 355 tool for clipping plant stems for maintenance or to gather flowers

greenhouse 355 glass enclosure that protects growing plants from cold

lap of luxury 355–6 state of excessive wealth and freedom from want

concede 357 admit

allegiance 357 loyalty

played for fools 357 deceived; tricked

Journal and Discussion Questions

1. What earlier material does the line "A creature as unquenchable as the sun" call up?

2. What do you think Katniss means by referring to herself as a "fire mutt"?

3. What do you make of the line "I consume myself, but to no end"? What end(s) could there be?

4. If Coin sent Peeta to kill Katniss, why would she now be keeping her promise to Katniss to let her kill Snow?

5. What is a "mental Avox" and what, according to Dr. Aurelius, is the cure?

6. How has Katniss's mantra changed since Chapter 1? Why?

7. Analyze Snow's comments. Is he lying and/or telling the truth? What evidence supports your conclusions?

8. What agreement is Snow referring to in the last line of the chapter? Did Snow and Katniss really have an agreement not to lie? Explain why you think as you do?

9. Summarize the loose ends you see in need of tying up.

Summary

Katniss hallucinates and/or dreams as she burns as the result of flames from the parachute explosions that kill Prim. Slowly, she recognizes things in the real world, and much as she hates to, she is forced to rejoin it, to accept the damage to her body, which—despite advanced burn treatment by doctors and her mother—is still scarred, and the loss of Prim. Coin visits and tells Katniss she saved Snow for her to kill. For awhile, Katniss does not speak, and a head doctor dubs her a "mental Avox." Although she doesn't ask, she learns that the Capitol fell the day of the parachute attacked, and President Coin now leads Panem. President Snow is imprisoned and awaiting trial. Cressida and Pollux are covering the war aftermath in the districts. Gale is dealing with the remaining Peacekeepers in 2. Peeta was in the City Circle, too, when the parachutes went off, and is still in the burn unit. Mrs. Everdeen buries her grief in her work. Katniss begins to wander and find secret spots, as she did in 13. Her mantra changes, acknowledging that killing Snow will be the end of the Hunger Games.

After a time, President Snow is found guilty and sentenced to execution, and Katniss's Mockingjay outfit and bow arrive. Then one afternoon she wanders to a guarded door, and is only allowed in on Paylor's say-so. It's a rose garden, and as she cuts one, she hears President Snow speak. He offers his sympathies on the death of Prim, and claims he was about to surrender when "they" released the parachutes, and credits Plutarch with the plan. Katniss recalls the weapons Gale and Beetee designed. Snow continues, telling Katniss that he failed to see Coin's design to have the districts and Capitol destroy each other and then step into the vaccuum. He says he was watching the Mockingjay and Katniss was watching him, and they've both been played. When Katniss says she doesn't believe him, he retorts that he thought they had agreed not to lie to each other.

Chapter 26

The Truth About Coin; The Vote; Assassination

Vocabulary

brainchild 360 invention
consummate survivor 360 champion at looking after his own interests
irrefutable 360 not open to argument
sauntered 360 walked in casually, without a great deal of effort
paranoia 361 state of excessive, unreasonable fear
speculate 361 guess
broach the subject 362 mention the topic
rat ... out 362 betray
rampage 362 act out in a violent, uncontrolled way
unkempt 362 not groomed: hair uncombed, unshaven, clothes rumpled and dirty

swathed 363 wrapped in layers of
metamorphosis 363 transformation into a new, more advanced and beautiful, form
repertoire 363 selection of materials the performance of which is rotated
ravaged 364 seriously damaged
inexcusable 367 unable to be accepted or forgiven
annihilation 368 complete destruction (*complete* before is redundant)
sustainable 368 able to endure w/ enough people
colleagues 369 people w/ whom one works
in lieu of 369 instead of

Journal and Discussion Questions

1. Evaluate the evidence Katniss supplies for the two scenarios of who is responsible for killing Prim.

2. Why does Katniss go to see Haymitch but then leave without an answer?

3. How is this chapter different with Effie than it would have been without her?

4. Answer Katniss's question about what would have happened to her and Gale if she had not been reaped as best you can. Provide support for your response.

5. How can Gale not know if it is his bomb?

6. Explain the rationale for each of the victor's choices in the vote.

7. When and why does Katniss make the decision to assasinate Coin rather than execute Snow?

8. Summarize the chapter based on your own conjectures, even if they differ from Katniss's.

Summary

Paylor asks if Katniss found what she was seeking, and she holds up the rose, and heads back to her room, where she puts it in water and considers the two possibilities: that the Capitol dropped the parachutes or that the rebels did. The evidence seems to tend towards Snow's explanation, when Katniss suddenly realizes that Prim wasn't old enough to have been in combat—that someone had to clear her or purposely send her, possibly to kill her and destroy Katniss. She concludes that she's being paranoid, but continues to consider it. She tries to think of whom she could trust to discuss it, and heads to Haymitch's room, where he lies, drunk, in a complete mess. When she says she needs his help, he makes a crack about "boy trouble," and she leaves and hides in a wardrobe, where she has terrible nightmares and is rescued by the guards and taken back to her room. She finds Haymitch with pills and foods, and then goes to bathe, whereupon she is greeted by her prep team. Returning to her bedroom, she finds Effie Trinket, who looks the same, except for her vacant eyes: she had been imprisoned and Plutarch and Haymitch had to make a case for her as a rebel to keep her alive.

After Katniss is dressed as the Mockingjay, Gale comes in with her sheath, holding a single arrow—the last shot of the war, and they stand looking at themselves in the mirror, as Katniss wonders what would have happened to them had she not been reaped. Katniss mentions that Gale didn't come to see her in the hospital, and he doesn't answer. She asks if it was his bomb, and he says he doesn't know, but she'll always wonder. Katniss considers calling him back and saying she'll find a way around it, but she can't. Katniss gathers her prep team and is brought by Effie to a meeting of all living victors. Coin offers them the vote on whether a final Hunger Games should be held to punish the Capitol without further depleting the population, as a way of satisfying those who want to kill all Capitol citizens. Katniss carefully votes yes, and Haymitch, apparently reading her intentions, casts the deciding vote for it. Coin promises to tell Snow about the Games, and Katniss prepares to shoot Snow. As she aims, she recalls her "agreement" with Snow, and changing her aim, shoots President Coin dead.

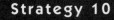

Strategy 10

Drawing on History and Mythology— Spartacus and Theseus

Directions:
First, read the information. Then, answer the question or questions.

Collins has said repeatedly that her story draws on the mythic figure of Theseus and the legendary figure of Spartacus. To analyze an author's statement about influences, you can gather information about the sources and then compare them to the work you are reading.

Spartacus

Spartacus was a freeborn Thracian who may have served in the Roman army in Macedonia. After deserting, he was outlawed, sold into slavery, and trained in Capua at the gladiatorial school of Batiatus. In about 73 BCE, he led approximately 70 other gladiators, armed with kitchen utensils and stolen weapons, in an escape, joined by other slaves. Not taking the rebel threat seriously, the Senate sent a praetor with new recruits, and he attempted to starve the slaves by blocking the main road to their camp. But Spartacus led his army behind them, seizing their camp when they fled. This success led to many new recruits, building up an army of tens of thousands.

The Senate sent a larger army led by two consuls, who attacked a subset of Spartacus's forces in south Italy, while Spartacus headed for the Alps. The leader and many of the force were killed. Then the consuls trapped Spartacus's army between them, not realizing that Spartacus now had a cavalry. With it, he beat them and captured all the supplies of one consul's army. Spartacus then defeated another force led by a Roman governor, and headed to the Strait of Messina, hoping to cross to Sicily. Failing, he turned north again and faced a ruthless Roman called Crassus. Crassus built fortifications to trap and starve Spartacus's army. Spartacus offered a peace treaty but was refused. He escaped the trap, but lost many soldiers in the operation, and his army split. Two other forces, led by Lucullus and Pompey arrived. The offshoot of Spartacus's army was defeated by Crassus at the Battle of Cantenna. Spartacus attacked Crassus in April 71 BCE, but he was kiled in the battle and his army was defeated.

Theseus

Minos, king of Crete, exacted tribute from the Athenians of seven youths and seven maidens, sent every year to be fed to the Minotaur, a monster half bull and half human, kept in a labyrinth that prevented escape. Theseus decided to end this practice or die trying. So he volunteered as tribute. In Crete, the tributes were shown to Minos, his daughter, Ariadne, fell in love with Theseus. She gave him a sword and a thread to follow out of the labyrinth. He succeeded in slaying the Minotaur, escaping the labyrinth, and returnning to Athens along with the companions he rescued. He later became king of Athens.

1. Look up the places mentioned in the mini-biographies of Spartacus and Theseus and make a map showing the locations and labels indicating their significance.
2. Write a paragraph comparing and contrasting Spartacus and Katniss.
3. Write a paragraph comparing and contrasting Theseus and Katniss.

Chapter 27

Return to District 12

Vocabulary

eruption 373 burst
fray 374 intense activity
too far gone 374 in too bad a condition
clots 375 thickens, stopping active bleeding
cold turkey 376 all at once)
ballads 376 song that tells a story
airs 376 short songs
expedite 377 finish more quickly
rag doll 378 soft, stuffed, floppy doll
pandemonium 378 chaos and uproar
ruckus 378 loud chaos
forsaken 378 abandoned
exoneration 378 official release from blame

collective thinking 379 thinking as a group about the good of the group
fickle 379 changeable; having different interests and loyalties from moment to moment
matted 383 tangled so as to become a mass, rather than separate strands (of hair)
pare off 384 trim
dust motes 385 tiny specks of dust
racks 386 causes great pain to
stoically 386 enduring w/out protest
rebirth 388 new beginning; revival; a fresh start

Journal and Discussion Questions

1. Reread the last three paragraphs of Chapter 6 (p. 84). Analyze them based on what you learn in Chapter 27.

2. What is the decision Katniss makes after considering facing her mother?

3. Do you accept Katniss's analysis of why Gale didn't shoot her? Explain.

4. Katniss's mantra has changed again. If you could speak to her, how would you answer?

5. What has been taken from Katniss in this captivity?

6. What shows that who killed Prim is no longer a question in Katniss's mind?

7. Why wasn't Katniss condemned for assassinating Coin?

8. Do you think Collins would agree with Plutarch's assessment of the human race? Do you agree? Explain your responses.

9 What does Peeta's choice of the first thing he does upon returning to 12 say about him?

10. What is the meaning of the title of Part III of *Mockingjay*?

11. Summarize the novel by either: a) drawing an image to represent each chapter or b) creating a title for each chapter to capture its contents.

Summary

Katniss hears Snow laughing, and sees that he is dying. She considers what her future holds, and upon thinking of seeing her mother, makes a decision. She deactivates her bow, and aims to bite her sleeve to ingest the nightlock tablet, but finds she has bitten into Peeta's hand. She orders him to let go, but he says he can't. The guards come, and the pill falls to the ground. She shouts for Gale, wanting to him to kill her, but he doesn't. She fights wildly as she is taken to her old room in the Training Center, now stripped bare. Taking off her Mockingjay suit, she finds that her new skin has suffered in her struggle. She showers and eats and tries to figure out if there's some way she can kill herself, but realizes that the Capitol, again, has that power. She resolves to refuse her medicine, but can't handle the morphling withdrawal, so she plans to kill herself with morphling. But several days into the plan, she begins to sing. As she continues, her voice improves, but she is managing to eat barely anything. After two days in which she has not eaten, drunk, or taken morphling, Haymitch enters, announcing that her trial is over and they're going home. Plutarch, now communications secretary for Panem, rides the hovercraft, too, but neither Gale nor her mother are returning to 12. Plutarch says that Paylor is now president. He gets off in 3, having expressed his hope that the human race will evolve from its self-destructive tendencies. Haymitch ransacks the plane for liquor, which accounts for Katniss not seeing him again. For weeks, she sits and eats what Greasy Sae feeds her until she finds a box with all the family treasures. The next day, she finds Peeta outside, planting primroses in Prim's memory, and she gets rid of Snow's rose. She learns that Madge's whole family was found dead. Buttercup returns, and they mourn Prim together. She and Peeta create a memory book of those who died. Katniss and Peeta "grow back together" and eventually, she confirms that she loves him.

Strategy 11

Directions:
First, read the information. Then, answer the question or questions.

As we discussed in the two earlier teaching guides, the **theme** of a story might be thought of as the story's point or its message. A theme is often a generalization about life or human behavior or values—true, but not a truism—an author's insight into the way things work that he or she wants to share with readers. Through its theme(s), a story moves from the particular (a girl named Katniss; a group of victors forced to fight each other, a rebellion against the oppressive government of Panem) to the universal.

The message of a story is shaped by the author's intention and purpose. Besides patterns in the story (which often point to the theme), there are certain parts of a story that often refer to the theme: the title, the beginning, and the end (or both ends, if there is an epilogue). An important character's first and final words are also likely to carry powerful indications of theme. In a story, such as the Hunger Games trilogy, that deals with complex issues, there are likely to be multiple themes. But it can also be fruitful to try looking for a joining of the plots with a single, over-arching theme.

How is theme different in a series than in a stand-alone book? In a series, authors, obviously, have more room to develop themes. But in addition to additional space, themes that repeat across individual books or are further developed in subsequent books may gain additional depth and weight, while there may also be lesser "sub-themes" that are important in a single volume but less important overall.

1. Explain how *Mockingjay* repeats, extrapolates, or displaces the themes of the earlier books in the series.

2. Can you identify one or a small group of themes that you think are dominant in the series? Identify them and tell what makes them stand out. Or explain what factors make it impossible to identify a stand-out group.

Writer's Forum 5

Comparing Treatments with Multiple Parts

Directions:
First, read the information. Then, answer the question or questions.

When a book series has been adapted as movies, it is natural to compare the book version and the movie version of the same portion of the story, as well as comparing the success of each vehicle overall. To do either of these tasks thoroughly, you need to employ both evaluation techniques and comparison and contrast techniques. Of course, multiple readings/viewings will make it easier to conduct your assessment.

Evaluation involves holding up something to a set of preestablished criteria and then judging it based on those criteria. In comparing two editions that both tell the same story, you would evaluate the main elements of a narrative—like style, dialogue, characterization, plot, setting, themes, and generic expectations (expectations about the genre, such as that fairy tales will begin with "Once upon a time")—as well as assess how well each installment carries out its part in the overall plot structure. Stepping outside the story, you should also consider consistency. Is the book or movie version internally consistent (in each title and/or overall)? Is the adaption consistent with the original, and if not, are changes made for what appear to be good reasons, and do they work? To aid you with a more in-depth analysis, now that you've finished the trilogy, a Glossary of Film Terms (pp. 71–72) provides an introduction to the terminology of film analysis.

Finally, you would compare and contrast the two editions, based on your evaluations, as well as assessing how each makes meaning and achieves its effects within the capacities and limitations of the medium used. Here are some other questions that would be useful to examine, citing evidence as appropriate:

- A movie lasts about two hours, so a movie adaptation of a book generally leaves out material included in the book. What, if anything, is omitted or compressed in the movie(s)? How did this affect the telling?

- A movie script may have additional material not included in the book, or may make changes in the book. What additions and/or changes do you notice? Did they add value?

- How did your imaginings of the characters, settings, and actions of the book differ from the way they were presented in the movie? Compare the characterizations and the plots carefully. Did the movie provide you with new insights into the plot or characters?

- Apart from the book, did the movie work as an experience in itself? Did it hold your interest? Was it worthwhile? Are the movies internally consistent?

- Did the theme(s) you identified in the book come out in the movie? If not, what message(s) did the movie give?

- Which did you like better—the books or the movies? Why?

1. Write an essay comparing and contrasting the book and movie versions of *Mockingjay* (2014, 2015). Was the split of *Mockingjay* into two films effective? Why or why not?

2. Complete your essay comparing and contrasting the Hunger Games trilogy in book and movie form.

3. An individual wrote the trilogy, while the movie was created by hundreds. What effects, if any, do you think this had on the results?

Writer's Forum 6 Writing an Epilogue

Directions:
First, read the information. Then, answer the question or questions.

The end of a book and the end of a series deserve your close attention because it usually is meant to round off all the rough edges, supplying all the details and plot bits not yet resolved, explain what needs explanation, put a final exclamation point on the themes, leave the characters in a situation of equilibrium (noting what has happened to all the important characters), sending the reader off feeling that all loose ends have been tied up. The ending should make sense of the foreshadowings and plot development that has occurred so far in the book, and play out the main ideas that have been treated in the book so far.

So, if the last chapter does this, what's the purpose of an epilogue?

An epilogue:
- is often a good deal shorter than a standard book chapter
- is usually written from the same point of view and in the same style as the rest of the work
- in the case of a series, an epilogue can turn from the concerns of the final volume and address the themese of the series as a whole
- is often set sometime after the end of the final chapter, giving readers a long-term sense of how life turned out for the main characters
- since it takes place far in the story's future, it can also give readers a sense of how actions, decisions, and plans played out over time
- may be designed to preclude speculation that the author finds undesirable or address elements of the story that turned out to be more important to readers than the author anticipated

1. If you were going to write an epilogue for the Hunger Games series, what would you include?

Epilogue

Directions:
First, read the information. Then, answer the question or questions.

Vocabulary

tedious 390 boring

Journal and Discussion Questions

1. How long after the final chapter does the epilogue take place?
2. What is the effect of Katniss's and Peeta's children being referred to as girl and boy, rather than by name? How would the message of the epilogue have been different if they were named?
3. What is the significance of the physical descriptions of the children?
4. Why does Collins have Katniss say "five, ten, fifteen years" instead of just "fifteen years"?
5. Why did Katniss find being pregnant terrifying?
6. Describe the role music has in the epilogue.
7. What is the significance of the children playing on a graveyard?
8. What is the book that Katniss refers to in the epilogue?
9. Analyze the uses of the word game in the Hunger Games trilogy, particularly in "Hunger Games" and this use in the epilogue.
10. Does feeling that it's "impossible to take pleasure in anything" seem to you to be an adequate and accurate description of what Katniss would be likely to feel on a bad morning? Explain why you think as you do.
11. Does Katniss's summation of why she has bad mornings—that she's "afraid it could be taken away"—seem to you to be a good and sufficient explanation of what would cause her bad mornings, given her experience through the book? Explain why you think as you do.
12. Summarize the chapter by analyzing whether Peeta's and Katniss's plan for conveying their history to their children is likely to be effective in helping them be braver, or whether it is naive of them to think that it will be effective? Explain why you think as you do.

Summary

More than twenty years later, Katniss watches her children—a boy and a girl—play in the Meadow. The girl was born 15 years after the last chapter ended, and Katniss was terrified when she was pregnant, but her terror was mitigated when she held her children in her arms. The girl, who learns about the Hunger Games in school, is beginning to ask questions, and Katniss wonders how she can answer without passing on the terror. She says her children live in a world in which the words of the lullaby she sang to Prim and Rue are true, unaware that the meadow in which they play is a graveyard.

Katniss says that Peeta is convinced that their strong bond and the book will help them understand in a way that will make them braver. But Katniss realizes that beyond that, she will need to explain her nightmares—their origin and why they won't stop. She plans to tell them that when she has bad mornings, on which she can't take pleasure in life because she's afraid what she cares for will be taken away, she plays a "game," listing all the acts of goodness she's witnessed. It is repetitive and can be tedious. But, she will tell them, there are worse games to play.

Strategy 12

Directions:
First, read the
information. Then,
answer the question
or questions.

The end of a series carries a weight that the end of a single volume doesn't because there's usually a lot more to wrap up, and this is certainly the case with the large cast of the Hunger Games trilogy.

Endings can be good, bad, mixed, or equivocal.

- A good ending would leave the protagonist living "happily ever after."
- A bad ending would leave the protagonist unsuccessful in his or her quest, seriously damaged, or dead.
- A mixed ending has some good and some bad: there is too much sorrow mixed with whatever joy the characters experience, making the end bittersweet;
- And an equivocal ending is an ending that deconstructs itself, either because the outcome is left unstated; it's not really the end; the creator(s) are leaving an opening for further developments; or because the creators are cuing the reader to a cycle.

1. Is the ending to the Hunger Games trilogy good, bad, mixed, or equivocal? What details support your evaluation?

2. What long-standing questions are answers in Chapter 27 and the Epilogue?

3. Which characters' current status is updated as the book draws to a close?

4. Why do you think Collins doesn't include mention of any characters other than Katniss Peeta, and their children in the Epilogue?

5. What questions did you have as you read the trilogy that you thought would be answered sooner or later, but weren't ever addressed? Explain whether you think these omissions are purposeful or continuity errors and tell why you've made these assessments.

6. One question that was never answered is why Cinna chose District 12. Write an explanation for his choice that does not contradict anything in the trilogy (you may add details that are consistent with what Collins wrote).

Strategy 13　　　Understanding Tropes

Directions:
First, read the
information. Then,
answer the question
or questions.

A literary trope is a device that has been widely used—enough so that many readers will recognize it. It may be a recurrent character type, plot development, setting, narrative device, or other literary technique (although these tropes may also be used in television shows, movies, and comics). Many tropes have nicknames in order to more easily identify and discuss their use, and Collins uses a number of tropes in the trilogy.

Poison Immunity

A character either takes small amounts of poison to build up an immunity or is the sole possessor of the antidote. In either case, s/he can share poison without or with limited ill effects, thus deflecting suspicion.

Cult of Personality

A heroic character becomes idealized and widely influential through the use of mass media and propoganda, making it possible to wield enormous power over popular opinion.

Big Bad

A single antagonist is blamed for all the evil events of the story, but is too powerful to overcome until the very end.

Archenemy

A Big Bad who is the protagonist's chief foe is also an archenemy and usually a character foil for the protagonist—someone who has character traits that contrast with the protagonist.

It's All My Fault

In this trope, a character lacking perspective and insight wrongly blames him- or herself for everything, and may also be seconded in this assertion by the Big Bad.

Outliving Usefulness

Big Bads characteristically dispose of those who no longer serve their interests.

I Work Alone

Protagonists have a variety of reasons for refusing to join up, some legitimate and some not. This can result in defeat or problems that wouldn't have happened if they'd only been willing to trust someone else.

Terrorists or Freedom Fighters

Freedom fighters—often ragtag and renegade—may look a whole lot like terrorists from the other side of the war. That they are fighting for freedom is understood to make any tactics acceptable.

Gladiator Revolt

A character is enslaved and forced to fight as a gladiator after being trained. After winning the character uses respect gained to incite a rebellion of fellow gladiators, providing a trained army.

1. Explain how each trope applies in the Hunger Games trilogy. If you can, name another work of fiction, film, or television that also has the trope.

Vocabulary

Look at each group of words. Tell why it is important in the story.

1. cold turkey, ballads, airs,
2. scuttle, parboils, backpedal, straddle, grating
3. maintenance, bulky, utility, sewage
4. pruning shears, greenhouse, lap of luxury, played for fools
5. poky, storefront, distrustfully, repellence
6. eulogy, freedom figher, oppressors
7. human shield, unquenchable, adrift, rawness
8. reptilian, decapitated, skitter, slithering
9. collective thinking, fickle
10. matted, pare off, dust motes
11. geyser, minesweeping, electromagnetic pulse device

Essay Topics

1. If, in Chapter 21, Katniss had sought a parallel in the plot, rather than a song to explain her perspective on the possibility that Snow would get hold of Peeta, what might she have chosen?

2. Summarize the appearances and uses of roses in the trilogy.

3. Summarize the appearance, purpose, and outcomes (direct and indirect) of interactions with mutts in the trilogy.

4. List the times when Peeta warned Katniss of an attack, attempting to save her life. What meaning do you find in the parallels?

5. What is the meaning of music in the trilogy?

6. Do you think the change in Katniss's and Buttercup's relationship is symbolic? Explain why you think as you do

7. What does Katniss mean when she says "the evil thing is inside, not out" (Chapter 27)?

8. Do you think Katniss will participate in Plutarch's singing program? Explain.

9. Compare the end of *Mockingjay* to the end of any other dystopia.

10. How does Katniss's use of the word *rebirth* connect with other material in the book?

11. What is the significance of Katniss's single arrow intended to be, and what is it, given how she chooses to use it?

12. Revisit Peeta's comment to Caesar (p. 23) about murdering innocent people.

13. Analyze the character of Plutarch. What do you ultimately make of him?

14. Why is it important that—in explaining why she finally chose Peeta—Katniss uses the phrase "what I need to survive"?

15. Looking at *Mockingjay* as the third act of the trilogy, identify the climax. Explain how it fulfills this plot role.

16. Analyze the chapter endings in *Mockingjay* as cliffhangers, shockers, or designed to have other effects on the reader.

Theme Page

Hero vs. Protagonist

1. Look up *protagonist* and *hero*. Is Katniss a protagonist? A hero? Both? Is Peeta a hero? Explain. Does Panem's assessment of Katniss differ from yours? Explain

2. In Bertolt Brecht's 1939 play *Galileo*, the following lines of dialogue appear:

   Andrea: Unhappy is the land that breeds no hero.

   Galileo: No, Andrea. Unhappy is the land that needs a hero.

How does this observation connect with Plutarch's statement about the human race?

Promises

1. The Roman orator Cicero wrote in *De Officiis*, "Promises are not binding which were extorted by intimidation or which we make when misled by false pretenses." How does this apply to promises made in the Hunger Games trilogy? How does it relate to the Choice Analysis Tool?

Lies

1 There is a Latin saying, "False in one thing; false in everything." Does behavior of characters in the trilogy support this?

2. In disclosing that he held an unauthorized meeting, Andrew Young, US Ambassador to the United Nations, said, "That was not a lie, it was just not the whole truth." Develop this as a defense for Haymitch with regard to his promises to Katniss and Peeta before the Quarter Quell.

Forgiveness

1. Henry Ward Beecher said, "'I can forgive, but I cannot forget,' is only another way of saying, 'I will not forgive.' Forgiveness ought to be like a cancelled note - torn in two, and burned up, so that it never can be shown against one." What types of wrongs are forgiven and (more or less) forgotten in the Hunger Games trilogy? What do characters find it impossible to forgive and/or forget? Do you think this is acceptable, or do you think Beecher is right? Explain.

Real or Not Real

1. Write an essay analyzing why discerning what is real is a challenge throughout the Hunger Games books.

Resurrection

1. *Resurrection* means "to restore a (dead) person to life." Trace the theme of resurrection through the trilogy.

2. The mythical phoenix, or firebird, at the end of its life, builds a nest, in which it burns to ash, leading to the arising of a new phoenix. In what way(s) is this specific symbol of resurrection pertinent to the Hunger Games trilogy?

Glossary of Film Terms

In order to gain the greatest understanding of a film, it is important to understand how meaning is made within the medium of film. This section will introduce you to some of the key tools and choices available to the filmmaker by explaining some fundamental terminology. The terminology will provide a foundation for analyzing the films in the Hunger Games series. You will find that not all possible choices or combinations of choices are used in this series. Just as writers choose particular words and sentence constructions depending on their subject and purpose, so the director, cinematographer, and editor choose shots, transitions between shots, and the sequence of shots in time from among a wide array of possibilities to create the style of the particular film and to express its intended meaning.

The Scene—everything that is viewed through the camera, how that "everything" is arranged, and what actions it takes

>   Décor—the environment of the action, including outside (landscape; architecture), inside (furnishings) and in-scene lighting (called *motivated lighting*), such as candles, chandeliers, etc.

>   Lighting—motivated lighting plus lights added specifically for shooting (*unmotivated light*); as well as the level and color of light contribute to mood

>   Space—indicates relationships between and among subjects and objects stemming from affinity, cultural preferences, and context

>   Costumes—costumes not only reveal character, but hint at the time and place of the action, as well as the context (e.g., formal/informal); activity (e.g., arena/home); and culture/country (e.g., District 12/the Capitol/the Arena)

Composing and Framing Shots—framing refers to placement of the camera in the scene and other factors (level, zoom, angle, movement) that combine to determine what is included within the frame of the shot, as well as what is excluded and whether some particular actor's point of view is being shown; composition refers to the relationship of the subjects shown within the frame and distance from the camera

Shooting—besides color, contrast, and focus, this includes such things as:

>   **Position**—what is happening to the camera during the shot. There are three basic possibilities.

>   Stationary—generally mounted on a tripod for the duration of the shot, the camera can move up and down, swivel, and tilt

>   Body-Supported—hand-held in the camera operator's hand, the camera responds to the operator's movement; attached to a camera stabilizer that the camera operator wears as a vest

>   Moving—can be hand-held or mounted; movement may be provided by a vehicle, a dolly, etc.

>   **Height and Angle**—position and tilt of the camera in relation to what is in the shot

>   Eye Level—shot at eye level, giving the impression of the point of view of a subject, often before/ after a shot of the subject looking

>   High-level—shot from above, to show point of view or for other effects, such as to make the subject appear exposed to attack or weak; bird's-eye view, a type of high-level shot, may be used to provide greater perspective on the subject's situation

>   Low-level—shot from below, possiby to show point of view or for other effects, such as to make the subject appear to be in a precarious position or a position of power or aloofness

>   Oblique-angle—shot with the camera rotated left or right from perpendicular, which can help to convey violent or confusing scene; also called *canted framing*

Movement—includes rotating the camera on either its vertical or horizontal axis, as well as zooming; it can be used for following, connecting, or revealing out-of-frame elements

Pan—side-to-side motion to either show the breadth of something or follow some action that is moving to the left or right of the camera or shows the spatial relationship between things

Tilt—up-and-down motion to either show the height of something or follow some action that is moving towards a place above or below the camera level

Zoom—controlling the extent of what is being viewed by moving towards or away from the subject or object (or zooming the lens). Certain distances have standard names

> Long shot (LS)—shot showing full extent of object/person at close to the height of the frame, and includes some of the setting

> Medium shot (MS)—shot showing about half of the object's height (a person from the waist up)

> Close-up (CU)—shot showing only a single detail of the object (a person's face or hands only)

> Extreme close-up (ECU)—shot closer than a close-up to reveal very small detail

> Establishing Shot—a wide shot that reveals the wider setting, shows spatial relationships, and may help establish mood

Editing—the assembling of shots into sequences by juxtaposition, cutting, and the addition of transitions, addressing questions of rhythm and pacing

Transitions—the way shots are joined.

Cut—a shift from one shot to another; this may be smooth, with matching between the two shots, or not; a *smash cut*, for example, is the juxtaposition of two dramatically different shots with no transition, intended to shock the audience

Fade—image slowly goes to black

Dissolve—blend of two images as one fades and one gradually appears

Cut-in/Cut away—shifting from a long shot to a closer shot of material that was in the frame or vice versa

Intercutting or Crosscutting—alternating shots of two or more separate subjects/actions

Montage—series of rapidly shifting images, usually not accompanied by dialogue

Reaction Shots—shot showing reaction to something, e.g., conversation or action

Sound—shares the distinction (but not the vocabulary) of lighting: diegetic sound comes from within the world of the film; sound originating outside that world is non-diegetic. Actors voices saying lines is perhaps the most common example of film sound. This sound can be turned into subtitles, thus, text.

> Sound Effects (SFX)—additions to the natural sounds of the location, made to imitate subjects or objects in the filrm, whether seen or unseen (church bells; dogs barking; footsteps)

> Music—can be diegetic (when Katniss sings "The Hanging Tree"), non-diegetic, or a combination, helping to set mood, or reflect on the action

Answer Pages

Strategy 1, Beginning the Second Book in a Series, page 11

1. Genre: science fiction or speculative fiction; Narrator: Katniss Everdeen; Protagonist(s): Katniss, but also arguably Peeta, Rue, the districts; Antagonist(s): the Capitol, President Snow; Inciting Incident: Prim being reaped; Reversal for Act I: President Snow's plans to take revenge on Katniss for her trick with the berries. Reversal for Act II: Rescue of Finnick, Beetee, and Katniss by the rebels; failure to rescue Johanna, Enobaria, and Peeta; and the destruction of District 12.
2. Possible response: The book will be the converse of *CF*, which was about President Snow's attempts to take revenge on Katniss; that is, *MJ* will be about Katniss's attempts to take revenge on President Snow.
3. Possible response: The title links to Katniss, her pin, Cinna's costumes, Plutarch calling her "the mockingjay" (*CF* p. 386—it's not capped in *CF*), so it seems likely she will become a symbol of the revolution.
4. Possible response: "The Ashes" could refer to the destruction of District 12; "The Assault" may refer to the rebels' attack on the Capitol; "The Assassin" may refer to Katniss in her quest to kill President Snow. It is not yet clear how they connect to the book title. Because Katniss was the "girl on fire," the word *ashes* suggests a failure, in contrast to *spark*. *Assault* might be the next step in the progression from the Hunger Games with child contestants to the Quarter Quell with Victors, so maybe a battle in a "real" war? Just as *victor* and *enemy* could have been referring to multiple people (Katniss or Snow), so *assassin* is ambivalent, and it's not clear whether it refers to Katniss or someone else.
5. The reference to Katniss's shoes and the appearance of her home in the Seam of District 12; the buildings (formerly) in District 12; the symbolism of the Victor's Village; the relationship between Katniss and District 13; who Plutarch Heavensbee is; the origin of the pain in Katniss's left temple.
6. Answers will vary. Possible response: Empowered by the resources of District 13 and (maybe?) successes by the rebels, Katniss will encounter obstacles (battles?) as she tries to reach President Snow's mansion in the Capitol in order to assassinate him.

PART I THE ASHES—Chapter 1, A Rose in the Ruins of District 12, pages 12–13

1. Possible response: Katniss's state of mind and physical health suggest that she will need to heal before she can be of much use in the revolution. Her distance from Gale after all that has happened, Peeta's capture, and Snow's ability to find her are additional impediments to her recovery and presumably, her usefulness to the rebel cause.
2. Students should recognize that all three books start off in or around Katniss's home in the Seam in District 12, and all refer to her home layout and her shoes. They should understand that the place that she considered her real home, the place that grounded her in *HG* and *CF*, is now gone, and the destruction of her home and District 12 mirror her mental collapse. In addition, the streets of District 12 present horror upon horror, and her home in the Victor's Village—having again been infiltrated by President Snow, as it was in *CF*—fills her with terror.
3. First, Katniss says simply, "I had to see it" (p. 3). Later (pp. 12, 14), she implies that she came to pick up particular remembrances.
4. According to her, she is responsible for suffering and death; Gale is responsible for rescue and life.
5. Her take is understandable but not rational. Katniss says (p. 6) that she "had set something in motion that [she] had no ability to control" (p. 6), but saying she set something in motion gives her more credit/blame than she deserves. The treatment of the districts by the Capitol laid the groundwork, the Gamemakers creating the untenable situation, and Peeta, Haymitch, and Cinna "selling" her story, combined with Katniss's volunteering for Prim, kindness to Rue, getting the medicine for Peeta, "trick with the berries" and the fact that she happened to be from District 12 all contributed to the fact that the Districts found her inspiring. People who already had rebellious tendencies (consider what Haymitch yells before he topples off the stage (*HG* p. 24), including the leadership of District 13—which had the intent to rebel but not the charismatic figure they felt they needed—adopted/made use of her as a symbol. Even if her threat with the berries had been purely a revolutionary act, which it wasn't, she would not be responsible, nor could she have stopped the rebellions or the Capitol's bombing of 12.
6. That she is not on the verge of a breakdown (p. 4) and not crazy (p. 15).
7. Answers should include: Being in the Seam at the start of the chapter sets the stage for recap: where she lived; the firebombing of 12 and the buildings that were hit and spared. Next, there is flashback to the decision about allowing her to return. A pain in her left temple leads to a recap of being hit in the head as part of her rescue, which segues into a flashback of the effects of her concussion and her hallucinations. Her technique for grounding herself provides more recap, including information about her name, age, and Peeta's current situation. Gale calling down to her offers the opportunity to introduce him briefly. Next

comes flashback to the horrors she discovered upon landing, while her memory brings back President Snow's words to her about her being the spark that could destroy Panem, which leads to flashback about the state of the mines and some statistics about the damage the bombing caused, leading to flashback about immigration to District 13.and then back to 12's lack of preparation for an attack, how Gale led people to the lake and Mrs. Everdeen and Prim treated the injured until hovercraft unexpectedly arrived to take them to 13. A flashback discloses that Katniss has been given information that suggests that accepting the immigrants was not all from kindness, but also from 13's necessity to repopulate. Walking around the square, she recalls Peeta's family at the bakery and the punishments in the square—more recap. Passing Madge's house leads to recap about her family. In her house, she flashes back to the desire for her to take on the role of the Mockinjay, and an introduction to Alma Coin, recap and update via flashback on Finnick and Beetee. She then collects mementos, which recap the most important items from her early life. She then recaps all the suffering and loss of life for which she holds herself responsible. Buttercup leads to brief recollections of Prim's love for him and her other pet, Lady. The rose in her room leads to mention of President Snow, but what follows is new information. The only foreshadowing is the suggestions of what Katniss might do with regard to being the Mockingjay and the idea that Snow is after her for revenge. The differences from *CF* and *HG* include that here she is much less detailed about her relationshps with Peeta and Gale and more focused on the District 12 history and what she's going to do about being the Mockingjay. She's been forced out of the life of a teenage girl by circumstances, so that romance has taken a backseat to political issues.

8. Alma Coin is described in some detail, and seems likely to be important. Fulvia Cardew is mentioned briefly, and seems like a more minor character than Coin.

9. Possible response: It explains her desire to take him as well as her relative indifference to his physical state. Her compromised mental health is an additional factor, as well as her terror upon finding the rose from President Snow. Their relationship had been improving with increasing trust—it is likely that Katniss may have undone that by the way she's treated him in Chapter 1.

10. When President Snow visited her in the Victor's Village in *CF*, Kaniss's attention was drawn to the strong smell of blood and roses, and pinpointed the ostensible source of the rose smell as the flower in his lapel. She comments (*CF* p. 21) that "it must be genetcally enhanced, because no real rose reeks like that," and it is this so-called enhancement that she is likely describing as artificial in *MJ*.

11. Possible response: It led me to expect that Gale's intervention would help bring Katniss back to a place of better balance and that she could look to and depend on Gale. So far, Gale seems to be on hand to do that, but Katniss is going it alone. Without the expectation, a reader might be less surprised that Katniss doesn't lean on Gale at this difficult time.

12. Possible response: Just as it is arguable for *CF* that the inciting incident is Katniss's trick with the berries at the end of *HG*, it is arguable that Rescue of Finnick, Beetee, and Katniss by the rebels; the simultaneous failure to rescue Johanna, Enobaria, and Peeta; and the destruction of District 12—all taken together, create the impetus or inciting incident for Act III.

13. Possible response: I expect that Katniss will make a definitive decision about being the Mockingjay and that there will be a showdown between her and President Snow.

14. Possible response: They were captured by the Capitol and are being tortured for information about the rescue plot, which they will be expected to know about, although not all of them do. Some will likely die.

15. Answers will vary. Possible response from very astute students: *He wasn't exaggerating or simply trying to scare me:* He was both exaggerating *and* trying to scare her—Snow says his problem began when Katniss did her trick with the berries. That is clearly not true. Evidence: District 13, with its stock of missiles and planes, existed before Katniss was born. Plutarch (and others) had created an underground years before to overthrow the Capitol (*CF* p. 385). [More evidence revealed in *MJ*: Snow has identified and killed many enemies (and allies) to maintain his power.] Snow intends to make her feel responsible for the current crisis by exaggerating her importance. His claim that the Capitol releasing its "grip on the districts for even a short time" would cause the entire system to collapse (*CF* p. 21) is conjectural and therefore—because it is stated as a fact—deceptive: another exaggeration intended to terrify Katniss into submission. [Spoiler alert: It is also proved untrue by the end of *MJ*.] Finally, the "inferno that destroyed" the part of Panem that was District 12 was caused by Snow's order. It seems more likely (as well as a more just assessment) that an inferno destroying Panem will be due to him than to Katniss. *Genuinely attempting to enlist my help:* Snow tells Katniss that she must use the Victory Tour to "turn things around," i.e., stop the uprisings. Evidence: Katniss recognizes in Districts 3, 4, and 8 a fury and desire for vengeance that lead her to conclude "there's nothing I could ever do to change this" (*CF* p. 73). If even Katniss—known for her poor abilities to grasp others moods and intentions—recognizes that she cannot fulfill the task Snow set for her, then

we must believe that Snow—savvy enough to maintain power for all these years—knew as well. Thus Katniss's analysis rings false through and through. Collins might have done this to continue showing how bad a judge of character and motivation Katniss is, but it is hard to believe that when she realized she'd been sent on an impossible mission in *CF* that she didn't question whether the man who sent her was honest with her. We should also take into consideration that Collins is attempting to show the confused thought of someone suffering from PTSD, though Katniss drew her conclusions on the Victory Tour prior to this, and one might think that she'd remember something as important as Snow sugggesting that they not lie to each other and then deceiving her. [Note to teacher/spoiler alert: The conversation between Katniss and Snow in *CF*—specifically, the supposed agreement that Snow and Katniss will tell each other the truth—is alluded to again twice and forms a critical link in Katniss's decision to assassinate Coin. Because of the evidence given here, the interpretation that Snow was telling the truth (rather than pretending to in order to sway Katniss into doing what he wanted—i.e., not doing anything more to exacerbate the likelihood of uprisings)—is undercut, and Katniss's reliance on Snow's truthfulness makes her trajectory and the climax of the book arguably extremely weak and/or not believable. See answers to questions in Chapters 25 and 26.]

16. Answers should only include elements/situations that Plutarch experienced.

Chapter 2, Peeta's 1st Interview, pages 14–15

1. In response to Gale's comments upon realizing that Katniss had found Buttercup ("Now I know why you had to go back"), Katniss says that she returned to 12 in case there was any chance of Buttercup's recovery. Possible explanations: Both Gale and Katniss are being sarcastic; Gale is honestly attributing a motive to Katniss, and only her respone is sarcastic [Teacher/spoiler alert: Later Gale will help Prim save Buttercup in District 13]; Katniss was being honest, and Collins is trying to show Katniss's mental confusion by having her present inconsistent accounts of herself.

2. Answers will vary depending on the story chosen for comparison. Possible choices include *Divergent*, *The Giver*, and *A Wrinkle in Time*. In each of these science fiction stories, like *MJ*, sameness is the result of some measure of control and those who escape or avoid control and act spontaneously and from individual motivations are often thought to be dangerous by those who are the same. The Samers usually aim to force those who deviate into sameness or get rid of them.

3. By having Katniss say that the reason she and Gale must go to Command is "sure to be another relentless Mockingjay session," Collins aims to increase the reader's (and Katniss's) shock at the real reason, which is to see Peeta being interviewed by Caesar Flickerman.

4. Haymitch came up against the District 13 prohibition of alcohol, and is isolated while he becomes sober.

5. Although Katniss feels inept and ill-prepared to care for Peeta, she saves his life, and he looks on her as a healer (*CF*, p. 306). With Gale, Katniss has none of the feelings of inadequacy that she had with Peeta, but her efforts are so inept that Gale pushes her away, saying if she keeps up, he'll bleed to death.

6. She gives them credit for having stayed alive and having rebuilt to the extent they have without outside help, as well as for their willingness to take on the Capitol.

7. Gale suggests that Peeta might have been tortured. It is true that, though he looks physically healthy, his reactions might suggest some low-level mental torture. The suggestion that Peeta would make a speech in return for being able to present Katniss as innocent of connection with the rebels seems very plausible.

8. Gale is in control of himself and able to manipulate his surroundings to serve him; Katniss has lost control of both herself and her surroundings :her mishandling of the pencils is further evidence of her fragile mental state.

9. Peeta argues just as President Snow did in his conversation with Katniss (*CF*, p. 23)—but somehow she fails to notice this—that continued fighting runs the risk of exterminating the people of Panem. Katniss's arguments, which are far from eloquent, are that they cannot go back to the rule of the Capitol, and based on the firebombing of District 12, they can't stop fighting. It is Peeta's words that lead her to see that the only way forward for her is to accept the role of the Mockingjay.

10. Foreshadowing: Peeta discusses what the war could mean—it's not clear at this point if this is foreshadowing or simply rhetoric (it's rhetoric); Gale talks about what he would do to win the war— it's not clear at this point if this is foreshadowing or simply rhetoric (it's foreshadowing). Some students may think that the fact that Katniss's inability to care for Gale's bloody nose (which he got interceding for her), especially compared to the happier results of Katniss's ministrations to Peeta, may be a hint from Collins that Katniss and Peeta are a better match. Katniss decides to be the Mockingjay, which may foreshadow a win for the rebels. Flashback: the fate of Bonnie and Twill; the history of 13 and Katniss's life there since her arrival; Fulvia's "wastefulness"; relationship development between Gale and Katniss since arriving in 13; [Students may include Gale's conjectures—though he states them as facts—about what District 13 needed

before they could take on the Capitol.] Recap: Peeta and Caesar, with intermittent recap and present time additions from Katniss, recap the Quarter Quell; Katniss recaps the history of 13 as she gives them credit; the images from the Games that flash through Katniss's mind.

11. Answers should only include elements/situations that Gale experienced.

Strategy 2, Recognizing Hidden Continuity Errors, page 16

1. Answer will vary. One key problem (which appears in Chapter 3) seems to be with the contradiction between Katniss's claim on the first page of *MJ* that she had to see District 12 so much that she "made it a condition of . . . cooperating with any of" the rebels' plans and her failure to consider that—given the granting of this potentially dangerous and certainly costly condition—she could just as easily ask for Peeta's immunity. It would have made more sense for continuity if she knew she could ask for it but couldn't think of how to ensure that the promise would be kept. The fact that this enormous favor was just granted makes her lack of knowledge about her importance in her conversation with Prim (pp. 33–5) difficult to reconcile.

Chapter 3, Mockingjay with Conditions, page 17

1. Students should use evidence from the two earlier books that shows Katniss's inability to act or lie to show that she is unlikely to make good propos (at least in a studio). Evidence that students may use includes: *HG*, p. 117 "I'm not good at lying." *HG* p. 136 'If you'd known, it wouldn't have read as real,' says Portia." *HG*, p. 274 "You're such a bad liar, Katniss. . . . " [Note to teacher: Students may point out that Katniss is successful in one lie that allows her to go get the medicine for Peeta in *HG*, p. 277 "Who can't lie, Peeta?" If this is brought up, remind them that Peeta actually figured out that she was lying and only physical force and the overpowering effects of the syrup carried her point, not a successful lie.]

2. Possible response: It seems very likely that having helped Katniss build her brand as the Mockingjay and the girl on fire that her taking that role had been Cinna's plan from way back. Was he holding out on her? It might be fairer to say, based on his actions, that he might have been cultivating her as a trusted friend in order (he hoped) to mentor her into the role, but not—the last time he saw her—believing her ready to take on the burden of symbolizing the revolution.

3. Answers will vary. We know that Beetee is involved in weapon production (p. 11), but students may connect him closely with electricity and not realize that he could design a bow.

4. Students should point out the difference in Katniss's and Prim's roles vis-à-vis each other; the sameness in 13 vs. the choices in 12; the difference in how personal possessions are handled (Katniss's ointment is confiscated in 13); the difference in local leadership in 12 vs. 13 (Mayor Undersee, who reports to the Capitol vs. Coin); the control of food (self-sufficiency vs. scientific nutrition completely controlled by the state); the difference in ideas about the value of pets; the difference in decisions about when, how, how far, etc. to hunt; the existence, or not, of a black market; the differences in the punishment systems.

5. Possible response: anything that violated their rules, and the lifestyle in the Capitol might have led the prep team to hoard food, waste materials, ignore their schedules, reject the District 13 clothing, etc.

6. • Katniss's choice to be the Mockingjay is complicated. She strikes a bargain in which she gets nearly everything she asks for on the first take (Buttercup remaining as a pet; hunting with Gale; Gale with her; immunity for the captured tributes), plus an additional request tacked on at the last moment (immunity for Annie Cresta), and she agrees that Coin's response to her condition of killing Snow is fair. But it can hardly be said to be a voluntary choice: Haymitch, Cinna, Plutarch, and Gale have all been hoping, planning, and grooming/mentoring/supporting her to make this choice, although they all showed more or less restraint in pushing her, some of them explicitly making it clear that they were leaving the decision to her. But since she has been terrorized all her life by the Capitol, to say nothing of being in the Games twice and receiving personal and detailed threats from President Snow, she can hardly be said to have a choice that is free in any meaningful way. In addition, at least on the part of Coin, the choice is exploitive: she clearly thinks she got the best of the deal, and she seems to be after power if the Mockingjay leads the rebels to victory.

• Katniss is motivated by the desire for Life, Liberty, and Happiness, for herself and all the districts; though she's certainly not clear that these things will result, she hopes they may.

• The level, quality, and awareness of information varies with the aspect of the decision. Coin sprung the explicit condition that she must perform or she and the other victors will be judged by the District 13 tribunal took her by surprise (although Coin did say that Katniss must perform in the meeting). But she makes the decision not knowing Cinna's hand in designing her look, not knowing exactly what would be required of her (and more that will only be revealed as the story goes on).

• Coin's condition makes it clearly a final choice, but it was anyway: the role of the Mockingjay is deemed so important to the rebel cause, that it seems impossible that Katniss can get out of it unless one side or

the other wins or she dies while performing it.

7. Answers should only include elements/situations that Prim saw/experienced.

Chapter 4, Prep Team Freed; Hunting; Coin's Assembly, page 18

1. Answers will vary, partly because this is a very broad question. Some students who may have disliked the prep team may be moved to pity; those who blamed them for not realizing that they were preparing children for slaughter may think they got what they deserved; and some may reflect about what this kind of extreme punishment says about District 13, for example, that it seems similar to the Capitol's treatment of the districts in its harsh treatment of those who don't obey its laws.

2. Students who noted a) the implicit threat in Coin's statement, "But you'd better perform" —a phrase that Katniss does not mention in her comments—and b) the fact that Coin left Katniss in Plutarch's hands are likely to conclude that there is more threat to Katniss than to Plutarch.

3. Students should reference *HG*, p. 4 and *CF*, pp. 6–7 to show that Collins uses the fit of Katniss's shoes to show her comfort or lack of it with her society and her role in it. In *HG*, she was comfortable; in *CF*, her shoes pinched because she felt constrained; in *MJ*, p. 52, the shoes are "broken in all wrong"—symbolizing Katniss feeling that being a refugee in District 13 "is the same thing as being homeless forever" (p. 6).

4. Differences include: their hunting gear is provided by guards (not hidden in the woods); they go out in tracker anklets and with a handheld communicator; they have a time limit, upon which their continued privileges depends; the fence between the living quarters and the woods is much more of an impediment; than the fence in 12; and the animals are not suspicious.

5. Possible response: Do certain acts put people beyond the pale, whether or not they had a choice, were brought up in a culture in which the acts were considered acceptable, understood what they were doing, or have changed since doing those acts?

6. Students should include Gale's taking responsibility for feeding his family, his dig at Madge (*HG*, p. 12); all his comments to Katniss at the Justice Building, including "How different can it be, really?" and "... remember I —"(*HG*, p, 40); and the story of how he and Katniss met (*HG*, 109–112); the kiss (*CF*, 26–7); the argument by the lake over running away or staying to fight (*CF* 92–102); Gale's whipping and the second kiss (*CF* 104–126); Gale's response to the announcement of the tributes for the Quarter Quell (*CF* , p. 179); Gale's contribution to the pre-Quell training (*CF* p. 185); Gale's appearance in the Hovercraft carrying Katniss to District 13 (*CF* p. 380–1); and the incidents so far in *MJ*.

7. Answers should only include elements/situations that Mrs. Everdeen saw/experienced.

Chapter 5, Prepped for Propos; New Bows; Propo Flop, pages 19–20

1. Katniss's recap shows us one way to view the plot of the trilogy: a series of situations in which Katniss is being used and manipulated by one person after another for their own reasons, never able to act as a self-determining person.

2. She finds it ironic that she has to be cleaned up in order to be damaged, burned, and scarred "in a more attractive way" (p. 59); that as a rebel, rather than a contestant, she can't look like herself, but needs to meet some standards (p. 60); that Fulvia can deal with unpleasantness on the screen, but not in real life (p. 61).

3 Possible response: Her environment and upbringing was responsible for a large portion of her appearance, behavior, and attitudes when she was in the Capitol.

4. Possible responses: It's bad design, so it's not consistent with the way they work with food or weapons or security or government, and there's no mention of another factor (e.g., temperature) that would make a longer sleeve desirable. This suggests that there is another reason, and one might be that Collins didn't want to discuss Katniss's forearm scar before Chapter 6 so she made the sleeves long to avoid having to mention it, making it a bigger deal in Chapter 6 when it comes up in her prep. This is consistent with her repeated use of a strawman approach to add more punch to events, but here what she's doing is allowing readers' memories of things to lapse.

5. Katniss has never before shown distaste for simply being seen with the "other"—whether it was Beetee and Wiress whom the other Victors laughed at or Mags, whom others couldn't understand. It's not clear if this is a change of attitude because Gale has convinced her (but that doesn't really fit with her observations about Octavia), a symptom of her PTSD, or Collins's way of making Gale's attempts at conversation seem particularly heartwarming, since Katniss, herself, is embarrassed by her companions.

6. Possible response: By including it as a flashback, the reader encounters events in this order: an argument, Gale attempting to make up for it, then another argument in the past about something that's more important, then a conversation in which Katniss recognizes that she appreciates Gale's honesty: that is, it alternates between negative and positive, rather than piling on the negatives and then trying to compensate with positives after, so a better development pattern for keeping the reader thinking that they might

yet resolve their differences, although Katniss couching Gale's choice as herself vs. Coin doesn't bode well, given that he's clearly becoming an insider in 13, as indicated by his communicuff and his peer-to-peer interactions with Beetee.

7. Possible response: She connects the conversation with Beetee's method of winning the Games and possibly her conversation with Gale at the Justice Building (*HG*, p. 40) when he said about the difference between hunting food and killing people,"How different can it be, really?" With both these things in mind, she is afraid they will apply Gale's strategy to people.

8. It is supposed to represent that Katniss has been in a recent battle, which is untrue, thus making it represent, on another level, the rebels' use of lies to gain their ends, making them similar to the Capitol.

9. Possible response: He is impressed. The teasing humor of his remark shows that he is recovering. [Note to teacher: Kill–Kiss–Be is a euphemistic version of a party and online game with a number of variations in the choices of action, including "Be introduced to," "Marry," or a four-letter word for "Have sexual relations with." The unexpurgated version is used by men to classify women. Alternatively, Collins could be inverting the James Bond meme that men want to be him and women want him (and he has a license to kill).]

9. They both convey that she has failed to act and is not (cannot) meet the propo planners' expectations (at least in this mock environment).

10. Answers should only include elements/situations that Beetee saw/experienced.

Strategy 3, Understanding the Meanings of Silence, page 21

1. p. 7 "and the Seam became so silent, people could hear one another's heartbeats."
2. p. 16 "We sit in silence for the rest of the trip to 13. . . ."
3. p. 22 "In the silence that follows. . . ."
4. p. 37 ". . . everyone waits in silence while I sit at the table and scrawl out my list."
5. p. 37 "I shut my eyes and start to recite silently, *My name is Katniss Everdeen. . . .*"
6. p. 40 "'. . . Peeta will be pardoned.' Dead silence."; p. 45 "A door swings silently shut. . . ."
7. p. 51 "We wait in silence until my mother finds us."
8. p. 53 "Silent, needing no words to communicate . . ."
9. p. 69 "The top opens on silent hinges."
10. p. 72 "There's dead silence on the set."

Page	Who or What?	Usual Meanings?	Situation?	Expected?	Contrast?
7	Seam	night, sleep in on morning of reaping	Immediately after the Quarter Quell	No	Yes
16	Katniss/Gale	mutual understanding	After visit to destroyed 12	No	Yes (minor)
22	Caesar after Peeta answers	host regrouping, pausing for effect	Live televised interview	Yes (effect: give Katniss time to reflect)	Yes (minor)
37	Those in Command	patience, respect	High level executive meeting	No	Yes (w/ "resonant" Katniss)
37	Katniss	getting one's bearings; grounding oneself; thinking	Mentally disoriented person in stressful situation	Yes (repeat of earlier behavior)	No
40	Those in Command	taking something in; shock; surprise	High level executive meeting	No	Yes (w/ earlier reactions(
51	Katniss/Gale/ Plutarch/Fulvia	disagreement; mutual understanding	Group with diverse backgrounds and expectations	No	Yes (w/ all characters' usual behavior)
53	Katniss/Gale	longstanding hunting partnership	Longtime partners engaging in well-known activity	Unclear because of rift between them	Yes (return to previous behavior after rift.
69	Katniss's new bow case	excellent craftsmanship	Examining elite-level bespoke product	Yes (all descriptions lead to high expectations)	No
72	Those on the Propo set	awe; respect; dismay; shock	Reacting to a take	Yes/No, depending on knowledge of Katniss	Yes (w/ meeting in command) p. 41

Chapter 6, Haymitch Takes Control; Heading to District 8, page 22

1. Possible response: The reader who has forgotten all of Katniss's failures with acting and pretending and recalls only her impressive performance in Command when she demanded amnesty for victors, may be shocked by her failure and more interested in the recap of Katniss's greatest hits. The reader who remembers the details and is waiting for her to fail might be engaged in wondering what's going to happen to all the promises (therefore, her and Peeta's futures) if she fails. In either case, the counsel steps outside the first-person narration and provides a chance to see Katnis through others' eyes.

2. Katniss does not agree to do what Haymitch tells her. She says, "We'll see." This seems like an obvious tip that she's not going to do what he says, and given everything we know about his and Katniss's history, it's odd that Haymitch doesn't respond.

3. Possible response: Knowing that he's aiming for a representative government like the one in the U.S. today makes me think more highly of him and puts his strategizing in a new, more positive context. I wasn't sure about his motivation before.

4. Possible response: The Mockingjay outfit makes it clearer that Cinna had plans for Katniss from a long time back, although Katniss doesn't count him among those who used her—which could be interpreted as an oversight or an exception because she and Cinna also had a true friendship besides the designing. It also sheds a different light on what he (and his prep team) were doing: not just making her pretty to go to slaughter, but to survive beyond the arena and to make it possible for others to survive in better conditions than the existing ones. The design of her outfit shows his creativity in another area besides fashion and branding: armor for combat.

5. Answers should only include elements/situations that Boggs saw/experienced.

Strategy 4, Justifying a Revolution, pages 23–25

1. Students should mention lack of equality between the Capitol and its favored districts vs. the rest of the districts; the inability of any district residents to live freely and pursue happiness as they see fit; the districts not being represented in the government of Panem; the judges (Peacemakers) in the districts being dependent on the Capitol (not the districts) for their appointment and continuation in office; the districts being plagued by "swarms of officers to harrass people," including in times of peace; the Peacekeepers' immunity from prosecution for their mistreatment of district residents; the districts not having trial by jury; the Capitol legislating for the districts; the Capitol having destroyed the lives of many individuals, and entire districts through firebombs; the Capitol has "excited domestic insurrection" in the districts. Possible response: Inasmuch as the districts of Panem were suffering from many of the same injustices as led to the American Revolution, not to mention the Hunger Games, their revolution seems justified.

2. Unable to participate in government, held in virtual slavery, and having to watch their children killed every year in the Games, the citizens of Panem have no defined route for addressing or petitioning the government with requests or suggestions and many are too terrorized to even try—and this is by design to keep them submissive and enslaved.

3. Possible response: Being ruled by an insane dictator (Snow), with no pretense of a representative system, a declaration would only show their hand and could offer no possible benefit. (And since there is no reference ot any other existing country or peoples, they do not have to prove their case to anyone else.)

Chapter 7, The Hospital in District 8; Combat, page 26

1. Possible responses: She is being influence by his mindset; she has lost her previous openness to otherness and now feels the need to label it.

2. Students should grasp that she is brave, efficient, persevering, practical, and confident.

3. Answers may vary. Some students may feel that Collins is seriously overdoing Katniss recounting her own praise, given the choice to use first-person narration. They may also think that the sections of the book that recap Katniss's greatest hits, which careful readers already know, are boring, and that the level of adulation is not ordinate or believable, given what Katniss has actually done. Some may go so far as to say that repeating Katniss's accomplishments over and over is not enough to convince them that a girl like Katniss could actually have the effect on a nation that Collins claims. Other students may feel that because Katniss has low self-esteem and an unrealistic view (e.g., she feels responsible for things way beyond what is objectively appropriate), the extra praise balances out her attitude.

4. **Pt. 1 of question:** Students should note that Peeta was the first to point this out (*HG*, p. 91): "She has no idea. The effect she can have." Others' responses to her—e.g., Prim, Gale, Cinna, Rue, Thresh, and all the victors who were willing to die to keep her alive in the Quell—have demonstrated this power. Some students may object that Katniss has shown enough recognition of her power (e.g., *HG*, p. 121 "I am as

radiant as the sun"; *CF*, p. 206 "I do not see a girl, or even a woman, but some unearthly being who looks like she might make her home in the volcano that destroyed so many in Haymitch's Quell."; *MJ*, p. 40 "They'll be granted immunity!' I feel myself rising from my chair, my voice full and resonant.") that it is not believable that she doesn't yet understand her own power. **Pt. 2 of question:** At the beginning of Chapter 5, Katniss recapped her relationships with power players and attributed the dynamics of these relationships to other people wanting to use her. Here, she recasts these relationships as all being with people who recognized her power (when she, herself, did not).

5. The propo shot in 13 was scripted, untrue, and required Katniss to act. The propo shot in 8 began with footage of life being lived without awareness of the camera and ends with Cressida's and Katniss's desires (to get back to the hospital) coinciding, so that when Cressida tells her some real information (that Snow just aired the bombing live on television) and asks for a response, she gets a natural and powerful speech.

6. Answers should only include elements/situations that Gale saw/experienced.

Chapter 8, The First Propo; Peeta's 2nd Interview, page 27

1. In both scenes, the television is about to be turned off when, just coincidentally, Katniss recognizes some upcoming programming that reveals something that is critical to the plot, which—had she not seen it—would change the entire structure of the books. Some students may think that doing this twice in a series is too much, especially since it's not believable that the announcement of the Quarter Quell card was not required viewing in the districts. They may also point out that it's quite a coincidence in the world of the book that Katniss just happens to see this message intended for her.

2. Possible response: To reinforce for both Katniss and readers how powerful her powers of persuasion can be.

3. Students should make two points: First, that they would not want her to see that Peeta is damaged because it will distract her from doing her job as the Mockingjay. Second, since Plutarch is one of the persons Peeta is referring to when he asks her if she trusts the people she's working with, neither Plutarch nor Fulvia would want to encourage Katniss to question Plutarch's motives and honesty.

4. Peeta's words serve the Capitol because he's trying to convince Katniss to stop the war by referring to possible dire consequences and calling into question the trustworthiness of the rebel leaders. But his words also serve his own ends because he wants to keep Katniss safe and in a situation in which she will not be punished as a rebel if the Capitol wins.

5. Answers should only include elements/situations that Fulvia saw/experienced.

Strategy 5, Increasing the Challenges/Escalating the Stakes, page 28

1. In *HG*, Katniss volunteered to join a fight to the death against children roughly her age (though some of them had been trained and most were bigger than she) to save her sister. None of them had ever killed anyone before, as far as we know. In *CF*, Katniss has no choice—she is commanded to fight and against victors, which means they are all older than she, all have killed before, and they are closely linked, while she is a newcomer/outsider. That she has allies is more Haymitch's doing than hers. In *MJ*, District 13 and the rebels in other districts are at war with the Capitol.

2. In *HG*, what's at risk is Katniss's life and the lives of the other tributes particularly Peeta and Rue). In *CF*, at first she thinks what is at stake is keeping herself, Prim and her mother, Gale and his family, and Peeta alive. But because she must fight in the Quell, she narrows this list down to Peeta. The rebels, however, have plans to use her as a symbol of the revolt against the Capitol, so we are to believe that the rebel cause is at stake. In *MJ*, both sides know that extinction is a possibility. We have no information that there is any human life left on earth outside of Panem, so as far as we know, the entire human race is at stake.

3. Yes, *MJ* follows the same overarching pattern of activity as in the first two books.

Chapter 9, Propos in 12; The Hanging Tree; Peeta's 3rd Interview, pages 29–30

1. Possible response: Meadow—there's not much directly connected to the Meadow except the fact of it being the landing site for the hovercraft. Katniss's home—forlorness (the missing roof). The Hawthorne home—irrecoverable loss (the twisted poker). The woods—violation (intrusion). The Lake—horror (Cato; "The Hanging Tree"; Pollux's reaction). Hunting Rendezvous—regret (distance from Gale); hope (partial raprochement); distance (discussion of translating hunting for food to war). Mellark family bakery—emptiness (what Katniss sees).Town Square—terror (recalling Gale's whipping). Katniss's home in the Victor's Village—returning calm (packing; choosing not to check for roses); tenderness (Gale crying).

2. Answers will vary. Students may say that they were confused by Katniss's interpretation, or that—as in many other cases—Katniss was reading into the poem a lot that isn't there (See Writer's Forum 2: Writing a Ballad, p. 31), or that they found it problematic when Katniss says "You wonder" because they didn't wonder that, and it took them out of the story. They may find Gale's comment, "Maybe I'll be like that man

in 'The Hanging Tree.' Still waiting for an answer'" (p. 129) more moving than the song itself.

3. Possible responses: Plutarch seems to be placed in the company of both Cinna and Haymitch, who—however much they wanted Katniss to front the rebel cause—really care for Katniss. It is the most personal thing Plutarch has ever done in any situation, but unlike Haymitch's and Cinna's gestures, it's not in response to Katniss's private self (i.e., their hopes for her to be alive and well for her own sake), but in response to her (unwitting in this case) public service to the rebel cause. So there is a definite limit to the similarities.

4. In *HG*, Gale initiates the sequence and Katniss replies "with equal verve," making explicit that they are equally invested in the "game," and—we may infer—their partnership. In *MJ* (p. 128), Katniss initiates the sequence, purposely throwing the berry high so Gale will have time to make a decision about whether or not to catch it and acknowledging that he may or may not choose to participate. Gale does catch it, but "at the last moment," and pauses before adding ("saying") the end of the line. So the "game" is completed, but it is a pale shadow of what it was in *HG*, which—given the recent arguments—may suggest to students either there's still a shadow of a possibility for Gale and Katniss as a couple, or that they've almost completely lost what they once had.

5. Gale believes that he only has romantic interest for Katniss when he is in pain. Answers may vary in analyzing his statement. Possible response: Gale is, in effect, putting the burden of the failing relationship on Katniss, suggesting that she prefers a certain type. He does not acknowledge that his strength is not simply strength, but tied to a particularly brutal approach to dealing with enemy combatants that Katniss finds somewhat horrifying, and that has something to do with why Katniss prefers him in pain.

6. Possible response: It is a sign that Gale is learning that he can (no longer) hold Katniss's heart, and so he is, consciously or unconsciously, pulling away.

7. Plutarch's interest in technology of war fits with his having been a Gamemaker, but the fact that Katniss mentions "moral squeamishness" as one of the reasons these weapons are no longer available, puts him (and by extension, perhaps, Coin) in the camp with Gale and Beetee: those who do not accept any limits on what it is permissible to do to an enemy.

8. Plutarch's "spasms of delight" over Beetee's technological success contrast sharply with Katniss's, Finnick's, and Haymitch's concerns for Peeta's well being. It reinforces his removal from personal concerns—the execution of the rebellion is clearly the first and foremost matter of importance to him.

9. Answers will vary. News stories should include the facts of what happened, as well as accurately represent Plutarch's and Haymitch's responses to the interview.

10. Answers will vary. Possible response. Peeta begins as he has before, talking about the dangers of war leading to extinction. But in his last sentence, he veers off and seems to be giving a warning.

11. Students comparison of the three interviews with Peeta should include the following: his (deteriorating) state of health; the topics covered; his words to Katniss; Caesar's role in the first two; the significance of the third being a co-appearance with Snow.

12. Answers will vary. Some students may think Peeta will be killed (some may point out the similarity to what happened to Cinna and suggest that it wasn't an accident that the blow to Peeta was broadcast).. Others may think that he will "just" be tortured more, and may point out that killing Peeta would destroy the Gale vs. Peeta tension. Others who think the broadcast was purposeful may realize that what is being done with Peeta is being done with an eye towards disabling Katniss.

13. Possible resonse: It's a combination of cliffhanger (what did Peeta's message mean) and shocker (Peeta being attacked on live television).

14. Answers should only include elements/situations that Cressida saw/experienced.

Writer's Forum 2, Writing a Ballad, pages 31–32

1. Conventional elements of "The Hanging Tree" include its use of outlaws, lovers, repetition and repetend, minimal setting, and rhythm and rhyme schemes. It differs in layout, in having little action, in using an unidentified first-person narrator, and in leaving a lot unsaid, to the point of being extremely cryptic, which is puzzling, given that Katniss's singing has a profound effect on Pollux, making it appear that we are intended to believe that they interpreted it a single hearing. One possible explanation is that 'the lyrics mean whatever you want them to mean,' but that is not the nature of ballads, which tell a specific story , so if that's what Collins is going for, she's created a problematic interpretive situation for the reader.

2. **Stanza 1, Line 1**: The speaker is not named or identified. We do not know if the speaker is male or female, young or old. The repetition of the question "Are you, are you" may suggest either urgency or intense interest in the answer. It is not clear if this is from desire for the person to come or simply desire to know the outcome of the addressee's choice. **Line 2:** "Coming" (not "going") suggests that the speaker is by the tree. **Line 3:** The tense changes to past ("strung up") with no time reference. We may assume that it is

more or less recent, or of particular note to the speaker and the addressee. "They say" may refer to gossip or a false accusation: there is no supporting evidence for any particular interpretation. The question ends with a period, not a question mark. Does this mean that it is assumed the person won't come? **Line 4:** Does "strange" mean unusual, supernatural, or bizarre? There's no evidence yet to decide. What would happen at a hanging tree besides a hanging? Is this an invitation to a hanging? There's no answer and no punctuation after the line to guide the reader in interpreting its relationship to line 5. **Lines 5–6:** The judgment that the speaker meeting with the person being addressed would be "no stranger" than the strange things that have already happened is puzzling. The preposition *in* in line 6 makes it sound as if both the speaker and addressee are going to be hung. "No stranger would it be if we met up" seems to create a link between the strung up man, on the one hand, and the speaker and his addressee, on the other. **Possible explanation:** Speaker is a criminal (or innocent person), addressing a confederate (or friend). The speaker has been caught and expects to be hung for a crime (or on a pretext), and is warning his or her confederate (or friend) of the likelihood of being captured, resulting in their being hung together, which will—whether they are guilty or innocent—be no stranger than the previous hanging of a man on hearsay. The question "Are you" takes on the cast of the speaker simply wanting to know what has happened: has the confederate/friend escaped? Or will s/he, too, be sentenced to death?

Stanza 2, Line 3: The speaker is again recalling the earlier hanging, and now relating something that *is* strange. Apparently the dead man spoke, warning his love to run away. This seems to parallel the action of the current speaker, so maybe the speaker is also warning a lover, altering the possible explanation a little. Also, "no stranger than a dead man speaking" is the equivalent of "very strange indeed."

Stanza 3, Line 3: "Where I told you" creates links the speaker and the man who was hung because the content of what each said—"called out for his love to flee"; "told you to run" is, then, synonymous. "So we'd both be free" seems to mean that the speaker, through death, and the lover, through flight, would both attain freedom. One things is puzzling: Given that the speaker apparently came back from the dead to warn his love to flee, we may wonder what could possibly happen that would be equally strange?

Stanza 4, Line 3: The first three instances of line 3 begin with the word *where*; the fourth begins with the homophone *wear*, but it's ungrammatical, so hard to interpret: the form should be *to wear* to fit ("Are you . . . coming to the tree to wear a necklace of rope, side by side with me"). *Wear* reads as an imperative in the middle of an interrogative sentence that ends with a period, so is extremely confusing. Possible explanations: Collins thought having identical beginnings was clever, didn't like the extra syllable, or both. This line seems to confirm the original theory, modified by the idea that the speaker is addressing a lover. There's not really much of a story here: the line does not clearly indicate that the lover dies, too. It's not clear what Collins hopes readers will make of this prior to reading Katniss's take, and that's a problem.

Katniss's Interpretation [Note to teachers: Although her explanation effects to play out stanza by stanza, Katniss is not sticking to the text. This could be intended as indication of Katniss's state of mind, but the level of challenge of this opaque and unballad-like ballad, as well as the extraordinarily complex differences between the text of the ballad and what Katniss says about it is far beyond the difficulty of any other passage in the trilogy. If "misinterpreting a ballad to fit her life" is the take-away Collins intended, it's very poorly executed, and likely to confuse nearly all students. Another possible explanation or contributing factor could be Collins' insufficient abilities as a lyricist.]

Stanza 1: Katniss says that "at the beginning" it sounds like a man inviting his girlfriend for a tryst, but the lyrics have no evidence for the gender of either party, no suggestion of a tryst other than joining in death, nor any suggestion prior to stanza 3 that there is a romantic relation between speaker and addressee. Katniss goes from "the man was hung for murder" to calling him a murderer, but the text has no evidence of guilt

Stanza 2: Dead man talking - no issues.

Stanza 3: "Where I told you to run, so we'd both be free" does *not* necessarily mean that the speaker was asking the lover to die, too. The repeated question can be interpreted as evidence of the speaker's intense interest in the lover's fate, wondering if the lover will be captured and die with him or escape and be free.

Stanza 4: It is by no means "clear" that the speaker wants the lover to die. And would it really be no stranger that two lovers died together—than that a dead man was able to speak? All the maybes at the end add to the confusion, and none are rooted in the text.

3. See pages 84–85 for a sample ballad and the explanation that follows.

The Miner and His Love

Mary Elizabeth

1 Cm / Ab / Cm / Gm

There was a min-er from the Seam just sit-ting down to sup,

Cm / Ab / Cm / Ab Fm Cm Bb7 / Cm

When glan-cing out the win-dow, he saw some Peace-keep-ers stroll up.

2

'Twas the head of them all who'd led the group the min-er for to

see, With ac-cu-sa-tions that he'd been the mur-der-er of three.

3

The min-er swore, his sis-ter swore, that he'd been no-where

near. The Peace-keep-ers in Dist-rict 12, they did not seem to hear.

4

His neigh-bors swore, the towns-folk swore, he had an al-i-bi. The

Peace-keep-ers were not con-vinced, kept up the hue and cry.

5

The "dead man walk-ing" told his love through a mes-sen-ger so kind That

she should flee, should run, should hide: to be free, leave the Seam far be-hind.

6

The mi - ner's love heard the mes - sen - ger's words, but she heard bet - ween the lines.

She heard,"Will you, will you come to the tree? Will you join me for now and all time?"

7

With - out a trial they took him out to yon old hang - ing tree, And

at the stroke of mid - night strung him up for all to see.

8

The min - er's love, his own true love, stood bold - ly in the crowd. She

did not hide, she would not hide, but called his name a - loud.

9

The min - er's love, she meant to be the last sight he would see. The

min - er's love, she meant that they should nev - er part - ed be.

10

They spot - ted her a - mongst the crowd. They hung her, too, on the tree. The

min - er's face was the last sight she saw. In death, they are now both free.

rit. -

In death, they are joined and free.

3. cont. Explanation: I decided to make the main character a miner and set the action in the Seam section of District 12. Picking up on "they say," I chose to make him innocent (this bit does not match Katniss's interpretation, which is not grounded in the text) and give him support growing out from family to the whole District 12 community. I invented a sister, and a lover, but all the characters are flat, and the focus is on the action. There are two times: supper and midnight. I did not use repetend, but I *did* use incremental repetition. The rhyme scheme is *x a x a*, and the lyrics are in ballad meter (alternating 4 and 3 stresses). The musical setting keeps the stresses on the strong beats of the measure, fitting other syllables in between, and uses Dorian hexatonic—one of the scales often found in ballads. The majority of words are single-syllable to reflect the level of education in District 12, as well as typical ballads, and some of the diction (*hue and cry, amongst*) is meant to suggest the archaic language of many ballads. There is some consonance (repetition of initial consonant sounds) and near rhyme—also typical in ballads (See *The Hunger Games: A Teaching Guide*, Strategy 19: Analyzing Lyrics , pp. 62–3 for more on rhyme). I played out Katniss's storyline by adding action—but since action is challenging for a dead man, I started the story before he was dead and also made the lover active, enabling her to interpret the miner's thoughts (though changing the verb of his question from *are* to *will*) and act on his wishes, bringing about the ending that Katniss envisions: the lovers joined in death and free.

Test, Chapters 1–9, page 33
Vocabulary
1. These words refer to the destruction of District 12 by bombing after the Quarter Quell.
2. These words refer to the epidemic that decimated District 13 and made them grateful for the additional people when the accepted the immigrants from District 12.
3. These words characterize elements of the lifestyle in District 13.
4. These words have to do with the weapons development unit in District 13 and its security measures.
5. These words relate to the bow Beetee designed for Katniss.
6. These words come from Plutarch's description of the government that will be put in place following a rebel success.
7. These words come from the replay of the first of the first propo in Command.
8. These are weapons, now obsolete, that Plutarch wishes he had available for the rebel cause.

Essay Topics
1. Answers should include at least some of the following: Katniss is still facing revenge from Snow—kept alive in her mind by the "gifts" of roses and the views of Peeta; Peeta is still trying to save Katniss; Katniss would still try to save Peeta (perhaps by killing him), if she could; there are strong parallels between the Games and the ongoing war.
2. Answers should mention the various degrees of freedom in her choices: first her terrorized choice to save Prim; second, having no choice about being in the Quell, but choosing to commit to save Peeta; and third, fighting when she was ordered to stay safe. Who she is fighting is also significant. In *HG*, she is fighting other underage children; in *CF*, she is fighting other victors; in *MJ*, she is fighting a cruel and oppressive regime in order to overthrow it and establish a representative government.
3. Possible response: Particularly given his explanation in Chapter 9 about how he thinks Katniss's romantic inclinations work, one would think Gale would be jealous of Finnick and feel that Boggs was comparing him unfavorably. It's not the kind of thing he'd want to address in public, and it would be difficult to bring up in private: given Finnick's state, it would sound paranoid.
4. Possible response: She's very similar to Effie Trinket: obtuse, wrapped up in her own view of the world and unaware that there might be any other view, and therefore insulting and invasive. In addition, she treats Plutarch like a god, acting very servile, and she expects others to do the same.
5. Students may suggest that Coin doesn't seem like the type who would let someone else be voted into an office above her.
6. Students should mention the plentiful sensory detail in the descriptions of: Katniss's walk through District 12 after the firebombing; her discovery of the rose; Peeta's appearance and mien in each of his appearances; the prep team when they are first discovered and Octavia during the first prep; the replication of the meadow in Weaponry; the hospital; and the scene, the lake house, Gale, and the mockingjays just before Katniss sings "The Hanging Tree" in District 12.
7. By now, we know that the question of what is true has pervaded Katniss's thoughts for years, due to:
   • her inability to interpret other people and accurately gauge their motivations (e.g., her attempts to understand Peeta's motivation in *HG*; the fact that Katniss has been forced to act in ways that may or may not belie her own feelings (e.g., Katniss's show of love for Peeta in the 74th Games);
   • the fact that many things that seem to be true in Panem are not or may not be true [only one winner

allowed in the Hunger Games, until there are two, then one, then two allowed; the reapings, seemingly the result of odds, but now known to be staged, with victors' children being chosen "too frequently to be just about odds" (*CF* p. 45); the rule being that victors are "out of the reaping for life," until they aren't (*CF* p. 175)];

• and the fact that people conceal things from Katniss for various reasons (Haymitch's apparent personal commitment to Katniss, possibly just a ploy to serve the rebel cause; Gale's personal commitment to Katniss, now seemingly wavering in the face of new possibilities for him in the hierarchy of District 13), Plutarch and Fulvia not telling her about Peeta, etc.

8. Students should note that Prim is "grown up" - training for a job that she's earned as the result of self-less and efficient work that she carried on in the aftermath of her personal horrors (being reaped; seeing Katniss go through two Games; the firebombing of District 12), self-sufficient, observant and wise, and able to provide comfort and advice to Katniss. Mrs. Everdeen is absorbed in her work and shows no signs of the weakness that afflicted her earlier.

9. The reversal is double-edged: Peeta's warning and his punishment (seen and imagined) for giving it. Although we have not yet seen how the reversal will play out in the second part of this book, which is part of what allows us to positively identify a reversal, we know that what Peeta does and what is done to him will move the plot in new directions as far as Katniss's reaction and the decision about whether to heed or ignore Peeta's warning and the consequences of that choice.

10. Answers will vary. Possible response: The healing provided to Katniss is minimal, merely making sure that her body functions, not addressing her emotional or psychological wounds, not protecting her from the outside world, giving her space and time to heal.

11. Possible response: The inciting incident for *MJ* is the rescue of the tributes by District 13, with the intent that Katniss should, as the Mockingjay, become the face of the rebellion. Like the inciting incident for *CF*, it happens prior to the action of the story, in the previous book. All three inciting incidents are related both in being tied to President Snow's rule of Panem—in *HG*, the institution of the Hunger Games; in *CF*, the game-winning strategy Katniss uses that puts in in direct opposition to President Snow due to popular reaction; and in *MJ*, the desire to build on the popular reaction to Katniss in order to overthrow President Snow.

12. Some students may believe that the words "it seems" are a subtle set up for a reversal of this opinion, another instance of the strawman effect that Collins has used elsewhere. [Spoiler alert: They would be correct about this.]

13. Possible response: Rather than simply saying that Katniss could see that the sight of Peeta hurt Haymitch, she says that she sees her "own dread mirrored back" in Haymitch's eyes (p. 133). The use of the phrase "my own" and the word *mirrored* make a much closer link than required to express that Haymitch was in pain, possibly signalling a shift from their recent antagonism to a new-found unity based on their shared concern for (love of) Peeta.

14. Answers will vary. Characters in Panem wield different types of power. The two characters with the most political power are Snow and Coin. Plutarch and Beetee have power in strategizing and weaponizing, respectively. Boggs and Paylor have power from rank, experience, and common sense. Haymitch has power from his understanding and experience (when he's sober enough to apply it). Katniss has the power of a sometimes charismatic celebrity; that is, others are swayed more by what she's been made to symbolize and her occasional ability to communicate forcefully than from a real understanding of who she is. Cressida has the power of the press: a journalist's power to tell a strong story and not only inform but also move people. Cinna had (and has, through his designs for the Mockingjay) the power to create brands and memes that capture the popular imagination.

15. Answers will vary. Students are likely to mention slowing down markedly or rereading "The Hanging Tree" and Katniss's explanation in Chapter 9 in order to try to make sense of them.

16. Students should understand that Peeta's warning and the assault on him in retribution are the events likely to drive the plot in Act II of the book.

17. Answers will vary. Student responses should be rooted in the story so far.

PART II THE ASSAULT—Chapter 10—District 13 Goes on Lockdown, pages 34–35

1. Answers will vary. Possible responses: President Snow has previously turned people known to Katniss into Avoxes and sent them to her. Now, he has done something that has—temporarily—rendered her as mute as an Avox. (Students may see a progression and suggest that Snow's next move could be to turn Peeta into an Avox.) Words formed from the root *silen-* appear 31 times in *HG* and 32 times in *CF*. The only time it is connected to a metaphor in those books is when Wiress falling silent is compared to the canary in the mines ceasing to sing. This instance fits with that, casting silence as negative and fearful.

2. Katniss visualizes Prim's decision making upon hearing the siren to figure out why she isn't present. She visualizes Buttercup's fur lining a pair of gloves to defuse her irritation with him.

3. Responses should include the following details: In a Level Two Drill, citizens are instructed to return to their living quarters. It is designed to remove citizens from the locale of a minor crisis, and it signaled by pulsing beeps. A Level Five drill involves moving the entire population of 13 to the safety of underground bunkers set up for extended living in the face of a dire catastrophe in the upper levels. Citizens are scanned at the doors, which are sealed when all are inside, and the exodus is accompanied by a piercing siren that cannot be mistaken for anything else or ignored.

4. Possible response: The formation of a queue at the Supply Station as soon as Katniss heads that way supports Plutarch's prediction. Although Plutarch is not skilled in one-to-one communication (at least with Katniss), he is an astute observer of human behavior.

5. Similes: "like raindrops on the window. Like wet mud on boots" p. 145; Metaphors: "I am Avox mute" p. 137; "sea of strangers" p. 143. Possible response: As she becomes more traumatized, Katniss's imagination seems to be more free-flowing so that she makes connections between disparate items that are similar in only one regard, as she moves away from the practical, straightforward approach to thought that she had when we first met her, leading to more figurative language. Answers to the final part of the question will vary: Students may find that the raindrops comparison works, but may think that the comparison to mud is not apt, both because of the texture of wet mud and because—while rain is often used as a metaphor for tears—mud on boots is likely to make students think of other things (e.g., children playing in puddles, gardeners, or farm workers in a barnyard) which breaks the spell and detracts from, rather than adding to, the sense of sorrow and fear for Peeta's fate.

6. Coin's initial response is measured and considering. Collins uses the phrase *mulls over*, speaks in an "even voice," and reasons her way through the situation, before coming to a decision. But once she decides, she acts decisively. Her second (first public) response, is still measured and is carefully worded (recounted in indirect discourse as "possibly made a . . . reference to an attack")—which could be both to avoid alarm and to refrain from giving credence to the interpretation that Peeta was warning them prior to having evidence to support that view. Coin's third response (second public), acknowledges District 13's debt to Peeta and their gratitude as well in the first sentence, before providing more information and instructions to the citizens. [Students may compare Coin's acknowledgement of debt and gratitude with Katniss's concern with these things in *HG*. They may contrast it with Katniss's limited expression of thanks to Gale in this chapter.]

7. The theme of debt returns in two ways. Coin explicitly expresses the community's debt and gratitude to Peeta very shortly after the first bomb strikes, proving that he risked his life to warn them. Katniss thanks Gale for saving her family's possessions, but does not give the act—or Gale—much thought. Students may point out that Katniss didn't even think about Gale until she heard his voice as he ran down the stairs with Prim and that she doesn't use the words *debt* or *gratitude* in relation to him.

8. Students may think that Plutarch is trying to keep Katniss from being distracted by Peeta's situation and focus her on her role as the Mockingjay, while at the same time exhibiting his poor one-to-one interpersonal skills. Katniss is first focused on his communication failures, but after her experience at the Supply Station, keeps his advice in mind (except for when she discovers Prim is not there).

9. Students should identify that *crooning* is a type of singing, and draw comparisons with other uses of music—particularly Katniss singing to Rue, and the ability of the mockingjays to create harmony out of little snatches of song—and the idea that art and nature are the sources of comfort and beauty in the world of Panem.

10. Answers will vary. Some students may think that the Capitol is brainwashing him. Students that predict that—in parallel to Gale, who has to decide if he's on Katniss's side or Coin's—Peeta will be torn between working for the Capitol (under duress or possibly brainwashing) and staying true to Katniss and his mission to keep her alive.

11. Answers will vary and students may respond in two different ways. First, students may link this conversation to the conversation between Katniss and Prim in Chapter 3. Some may find Prim's mature insight and understanding to be without sufficient underpinnings, especially when she is 13 years old. Second, students may respond to the content of the statement and either a) consider what might be done to Peeta in order to break Katniss or b) posit that this should have been obvious to Katniss from past history (posting Darius in her suite after making him an Avox; killing Cinna in front of her; etc.) and because Finnick warned her on the hovercraft on the way to District 13 (*CF* p. 388).

12. Answers should only include elements/situations that Prim saw/experienced.

Chapter 11, Katniss Breaks; Rescue Mission Pt. 1, page 36

1. She comes to understand that Peeta will be tortured for any public action on her part, kept alive, but made to continually suffer.
2. There are four more bunker bombs dropped over the course of three more days, seemingly planned to keep 13 in lockdown. The damage, while serious, is not devastating, which makes sense since the Capitol wants to acquire 13's military technology.
3. Answers will vary. Some students may find the extended metaphor to be fruitful. Other students may think that comparing a cat trick described as "clever" and "delightful" entertainment to Peeta's plight doesn't work and that it trivializes Peeta's situation and Katniss's suffering, presently and were Peeta to die. Others may think it seems contrived, and may note that it is another situation in which Collins forces an interpretation rather than allowing readers to infer meaning.
4. Answers will vary. Students may point out that since Katniss—who is characteristically not adept at concealing her feelings—was a) glaring at Finnick and b) described herself at the time as "furious" because his saving Peeta meant she cannot kill Finnick, it seems very unlikely that he would be able in that moment to infer that she loved Peeta.
5. Answers will vary. Students may point out that tying knots does not demand a lot of intense concentration and focus, so it won't keep one from thinking, making it unlikely to serve well as a distraction.
6. Presumably, 13 has been "off the air" for the four days of the lockdown, so needs to get back with fresh material. Also, they need to combat whatever propaganda the Capitol has been airing about the attack, show that they've been damaged but are undaunted, still have military prowess, and that the Mockingjay lives.
7. Answers will vary. Possible responses: a) It shows how distant Gale and Katniss are that he could think this. b) It is such a ludicrous conclusion that it diminishes Gale to have him think it and helps move the reader towards accepting that Katniss will choose Peeta.
8. Answers will vary. Students may suggest that it would be odd for the part title to refer to something that was over in the second chapter of the part. They may also point to the use of titles capable of multiple interpretations ("The Victor" in *HG*; "The Enemy" in *CF*) and suggest that this title is likely similar, so we can't know what it means until we've read all of the chapters in the part.
9. Answers will vary. Students may think that someone significant will die.
10. Answers should only include elements/situations that Finnick saw/experienced.

Writer's Forum 2, Writing an Extended Metaphor, page 37

1. Students should equate Buttercup and Katniss, the light being on with Peeta being alive, the position of the light in relation to Buttercup with Peeta's location in relation to Katniss. Though Katniss does not mention it, students may point out that Katniss manipulating the light to make Buttercup crazy equates with President Snow torturing Peeta to incapacitate Katniss.
2. Answers will vary. Students should use metaphor to provide insight by showing several points of comparison in a pleasing way.

Chapter 12, Rescue Mission Pt. 2; Peeta Awakens, page 38

1. Collins has presented three passages in which Katniss has focused on Gale's and Peeta's hands in *CF* pp. 27, 95, and 161), and this laid groundwork for the sentence in question to give it a depth of meaning.
2. Possible response: It increased both my understanding of his use of alcohol and my sympathy for him. It also increased my respect for his allowing himself to care about Katniss and Peeta and invest in them.
3. Both the story about Peeta giving Katniss the bread (*HG* pp. 26–33) and the fact that Finnick traded in secrets (*CF* p. 210) were mentioned earlier (examples of the Chekhov's gun trope).
4. Answers may vary. Possible response: Both the legendary Roman General Gaius Marcius Coriolanus and Coriolanus, the title character in one of Shakespeaare's tragedies, are notable for betraying both their friends and their enemies. This characteristic ties them to Coriolanus Snow, who did the same.
5. Finnick begins by explaining his situation after winning the Games—he was prostituted by President Snow, submitting in order to save those he loved from death. He worked out a way to have his "patrons" pay him in secrets—which they felt were safe with him because he wasn't in a position to tell anyone. He recounts some secrets about prominent Capitol citizens, leading up to revelations about President Snow, chiefly that he used poison to clear his political path of foes, as well as potential rivals among his friends. It was a failure of his antidote that led to the mouth sores that make him smell of blood and his use of genetically modified roses to try to cover up that smell.
6. Answers will vary. Some students may have suspected a strawman, while others might not.

7. Answers will vary. Students may predict that Katniss will despair; that she will turn to Gale for consolation; that she will try to help Peeta; or that she will try to get as far away from him as she can because this turn of events is so painful.

8. Answers should only include elements/situations that Haymitch saw/experienced

Chapter 13, Katniss Recovers; Beetee and Gale; Delly and Peeta, page 39

1. Students should expand on the very clear switch from Katniss providing the physical requirements that Prim needed to stay alive to Prim providing the emotional support and insight that Katniss needs to deal with her current situation, as well as nursing.

2. Possible response: Plutarch's view is pragmatic and "big picture." He is right that Peeta's situation is better and more promising simply because he has been rescued, but he knew Peeta as a gamemaker knows a contestant, not as a friend, not as someone who loved him, so he may not even fully realize what has been lost, possibly forever.

3. Students may note that the second doesn't seem to follow from the first. It's understandable that Gale didn't wish to disturb her when he slipped into her hospital room, but after she gets Beetee's and Gale's attention in
, why doesn't Gale greet her, ask after her recovery, or anything? Gale doesn't even speak for a whole page—it's all Katniss and Beetee until Gale answers her concerns about the ethical appropriateness of their approach, and then his answer is one that Katniss brands as "cruel." Does he know from the start that she'll disapprove? Does he feel that—given his insight into Katniss's preference for people in pain (p. 130), Peeta will have all of Katniss's attention and he doesn't stand a chance? We don't know, because Collins doesn't allow Gale to give voice to his thoughts and feelings or Katniss to consider them. Given Collins's tendency to overdetermine the reader's understanding of everything, this is a little surprising. It may, again, be a way of distancing the reader from Gale in light of Katniss's eventual choice of Peeta.

4. Students may scratch their heads over this. In retrospect, students may find that it portends Katniss and Buttercup being left to comfort each other after Prim's death.

5. Possible response: Katniss seems to differentiate (and Beetee and Gale do not) between soldiers killing soldiers and hunters killing game, on the one hand, and the development of weapons that both clearly target civilians, and taking advantage of love and compassion to kill. Since Katniss is not that articulate, providing instances, but not stating a position, students may feel some uncertainty in explaining her view. Students may note that juxtaposing Beetee and Gale on the one hand with Delly on the other may be a purposeful choice on Collins's part to express a condemnation of what Beetee and Gale are doing.

6. Students should identify that Delly is kind, generous in her assessment of others (and/or not very analytical), warm, extroverted, and compassionate.

7. The mutts are genetically engineered tools of the Capitol, intended to hurt citizens of the Districts and programmed to destroy them: that is, Katniss is not a person, she is a Capitol-controlled means of destruction.

8. Answers should only include elements/situations that Delly saw/experienced

Writer's Forum 3, Writing a Definition, page 40

1. Answers will vary. Students should take into account not only what Beetee says, but also Katniss's distinction between being deranged and being hijacked, and the distinction between hijacking and fear conditioning (hijacking is a subset of fear conditioning) and between hijacking and brainwashing.

Chapter 14, District 2 with Gale and a Death Trap, page 41

1. In Chapter 3, in a thought that took root in *CF*, Katniss makes a deal with Coin as part of her agreement to become the Mockingjay that includes a 50–50 chance of having the opportunity to kill President Snow. In Chapter 9, Gale first presents his theory about what's behind Katniss's romantic interest, and he extends that theory in Chapter 14. And in Chapter 13, we see Beetee and Gale working to transform Gale's hunting traps into traps for humans, and that, too, is played out here, as Gale compares the Nut to a wild dog den, and proposes destroying everyone inside along with the stronghold's value to the Capitol.

2. Plutarch lies, probably to try to keep Katniss thinking positively so she'll be able to carry out her mockingjay duties. Haymitch is truthful, therefore less hopeful. Given their characters and relationship to Peeta, this is as expected.

3. It's arguable that someone who empties her mind and concentrates on sensations is objectifying the person she is kissing.

4. Students should contrast Peeta's positive attraction to Katniss with Gale's jealousy of Darius teasing her as well as Peeta's single-minded devotion to Katniss with Gale's wider experience with other girls before

(or after?) deciding Katniss was special.

5. Students' chronologies should start before the rebellion, under Capitol control after the Dark Days, and since the rebellion.

6. Answers will vary. Some students may believe that given the weight given to Prim's opinions and insights, this may, indeed, be the key to Peeta's recovery—to whatever degree he does recover.

7. Answers will vary. Some students may think that the only way to fight someone like Snow is to employ his (dirty) tactics against him, as Gale seems to think. Others may find it reprehensible to destroy lives unnecessarily.

8. Answers should only include elements/situations that Gale saw/experienced.

Strategy 6, Analyzing Choices, pages 42–43

1. Students may say that Katniss's choice combines elements of a terrorized choice (due to her history at the hands of the Capitol and President Snow), a constrained choice (within District 13), and bargaining. Her role as the Mockingjay can be seen as seeking after life, liberty, and happiness for herself and the districts, but while the killing of President Snow would also tend towards those ends, students may argue that the choice analysis tool doesn't have a means to differentiate seeking goods in a positive way or through violence or war except in the italicized note below Part 2. Katniss's information about what is entailed is partial—no one can know exactly what will be required because it's dictated by the circumstances of the war. It seems that what she knows is true, so far, and Coin's ultimatum has made it clear that she is not a blind believer in Katniss. Katniss's choice is an all-in commitment, especially given Coin's ultimatum.

2. Answers will vary. Possible response: In Part 1, it seems that being hijacked should either put one at the opposite pole of free choice, or—because the hijacked person seemingly does not have a choice—possibly in a category all it's own. In Part 2, the hijacked person's own desires are replaced with imposed desires of another. Their information is false, and they are mistaken in their level of awareness, taking lies as truth. Part 4 depends on circumstance, not the state of being hijacked. For example, if Peeta had succeeded in strangling Katniss, that would have been final. His yelling at Delly was a choice that could be apologized for or retracted. One of the things that makes it hard to decide where/how to fit in hijacking is that Peeta seems to have broken through the hijacking in order to warn District 13 about the bombings, raising the question of whether some voluntary action is still possible.

Chapter 15, The Mountain Falls; Katniss Is Shot, page 44

1. **BRAINS: Beetee** points out that most of the people in the Nut are not Capitol citizens, but workers from 2. He notes that President Coin needs a chance to give her point of view. And he reiterates Peeta's point about the importance of ensuring enough people survive so that the country doesn't kill itself off. **Gale** says that citizens of 2 who have served the Capitol are no longer trustworthy. He compares the situation of those in the Nut to his and Katniss's fathers and those who were firebombed in District 12 and accuses 2 of complicity with the Capitol. He points out that in 12, children were burned to death. He questions if the others, hesitating from concern that the enemies will suffer for awhile before they die. He admits his willingness to kill the rebels spies within the Nut to achieve its shutdown and adds that if he were there, he would welcome sacrificing his life for the cause. **SOLDIERS: Lyme** says that those in the Nut should have the chance to surrender. **Boggs** suggests mitigating Gale's plan by leaving the train tunnel open for escape to the square, where rebel troops will be waiting. In response to Gale's question, Boggs says that the rebels will be heavily armed and take those who escape prisoner. **MOCKINGJAY: Katniss** draws a comparison between collapsing the Nut and the mining accident that killed hers and Gale's fathers. She points out that the people in the Nut may have been coerced or be their against their will or be rebel spies.

2. Possible response: Katniss had accused him of being on Coin's side, rather than hers, and here he seems to think that he and Coin think alike to the point that he overrates her endorsement of his view: Coin actually goes with Boggs's version of Gale's plan, which leaves the train tunnel as an escape route.

3. Answers will vary. Possible response: The five invocations of Peeta and his take on things in the chapter (both Beetee and Katniss bring up Peeta in opposition to Gale's views and plan), Gale's prideful assumption that Coin will agree with him, and Gale's intense anger and rudeness as he states his case both make Gale seem like an unsuitable partner for anyone and remind readers of how, as Katniss has seen more of the world, she has come to think more like "the old Peeta" and differently from Gale.

4. Her current situation brings back memories of the mining accident that killed her father; Beetee refers to Peeta's argument in one of his interviews; Katniss recalls the last time she was at the Justice Building on the Victory Tour; Haymitch tells her that they played her rendition of "The Hanging Tree" for Peeta, and Peeta recollected Mr. Everdeen singing it; Katniss recalls some of the tributes from the Seventy-fourth

Hunger Games in her speech and—at Haymitch's urging—recalls the question of who is the enemy that was so important in *CF*.

5. Students should recognize that Katniss takes this as the first sign of her mother's collapse into depression—that, hearing of the accident, she did not go immediately to find and care for her children.

6. Haymitch reports that seeing a clip of Katniss singing "The Hanging Tree" did not result in Peeta going into a rant, but in having a connected memory of hearing her father sing the song when he was young and waiting to hear if the birds would stop singing (apparently they did).

7. Answers will vary. Some students may think the man with the gun whom Katniss was confronting shot her. Others may think Capitol soliders shot her. Others may not know. [It's not clear.]

8. Possible response: It could be a critique of a culture in which events are only made real by being digitized and shared.

9. Answers should only include elements/situations that Gale saw/experienced.

Strategy 7, Analyzing Persuasive Techniques, page 45

1. a. Gale employs guilt by association in his accusation against citizens of 2 who served the Capitol. Ignoring principle, he argues that Snow did it in 12 and makes a broader ad hominem attack against citizens of 2. He then fails to control his tone, yelling an appeal to emotion. His response to Katniss is another ad hominem attack, implying that the others in the discussion are too queasy about suffering to make the "right" decision. When Katniss asks him a question, he clarifies his position, and then put's himself in the shoes of those in the Nut. b. Katniss makes a false analogy between what is presumably an accident and a choice that is an act of war. She then engages in choice analysis, and asks a clarifying question. c. Beetee is careful to moderate his tone as he makes an important distinction. He refers to protocol for the situation and appeals to authority in citing Peeta's argument in his interview d. Boggs suggests a compromise. In response to Gale's question, Boggs clarifies his position. e. Lyme does not cite a principle, but seems to be speaking from one.

2. Katniss begins by clarifying who she is. When asked by the armed man she faces for a reason for him not to kill her, she puts herself in his shoes and says she can't. She refers to the big picture (2 firebombed 12; 12 blew up the Nut), overgeneralizes ("we have every reason to kill each other"), and immediately offers a compromise by putting down her weapon. She them makes a series of appeals to emotion by mentioning Cato and Clove and Lyme, and appealing to the solidarity of miners, finishing with an extension of the compromise of putting down her bow, but inviting those fleeing the Nut to join the rebellion.

Chapter 16, Finnick's Wedding; Meeting with Peeta, page 46

1. Students should recognize that in *HG*, Chapter 15, in which Katniss and Rue form an alliance, and Chapter 20, in which Katniss tells the story of Prim's goat, are both markedly lighter than the other material. In *CF*, Chapter 16, in which Katniss and Peeta are checking out potential allies, is the lightest portion. (There are other brief sections of humor or friendly relations.) In *MJ*, Chapter 16 is it (so far). Possible rationale: The material in Chapter 15/16 is around the halfway point of the story, and gives the reader a chance to get to know the characters better in a less threatening environment as well as creating contrast with the next terrifying thing that happens.

2. Plutarch is making a propo of the wedding, playing on the bread and circuses idea, by showing 13 holding a genuine celebration at a time when the Capitol no longer has the wherewithal to do so.

3. They are adversarial roommates, with Johanna "stealing" Katniss's morphling, and Katniss allowing her to. They are honest, but not friendly.

4. Answers will vary. Students may think that dancing is so minor that setting it up isn't important. Alternatively, they may feel that Collins has created an expectation that there would be groundwork laid wherever possible rather than introducing a new characterizing feature of District 12 residents after 991 pages.

5. *Panem et Circenses* is a Latin phrase meaning "Bread and Circuses." It means that the citizens give up their political rights and responsibilities in exchange for being fed and entertained. The Capitol was fragile in that it relied on the districts for all the supplies necessary to provide its Bread and Circuses, and when the districts rebelled, it could no longer do so, thus losing its power over the Capitol citizens, who—unlike residents of the districts—have no history of nor ability to do without, being completely unused to any hardship.

6. The fact that Katniss thinks that Gale's argument could be used to justify the Hunger Games suggests that this is a more important disagreement than any they had had previously, and shows a significant break in their relationship. Students may note that Collins keeps readers from focusing on the implications for the Gale/Peeta question, by (awkwardly) transitioning to a discussion of Katniss's rehabilitation.

7. It is the first time in the series that they have done something fun together. Peeta and Katniss worked on the Family Book; Gale and Katniss teased each other while hunting; but never before have we seen Katniss and Prim have fun.

8. In Chapter 14 of *CF* (p. 189), expecting never to see her family or Gale again, she consciously ends her mourning for home and says goodbye to them, expecting never to see them again, and hoping never to be distracted from her mission to save Peeta by thought of them.

9. The chapter begins with Katniss dreaming of Peeta telling her that he would stay with her (and love her) always, and ends with her understanding that he now sees her for what she is and cannot possibly ever care for her again.

10. Answers should only include elements/situations that Peeta saw/experienced.

Strategy 8: Understanding Dystopias, page 47

1. The Hunger Games trilogy has so many of the attributes of a dystopia, that it should be treated as one.
2. Possible response: Collins is criticizing reality television, the entertainment industry, the vicarious thrills that many people in our culture live for, and the superficiality connected with it all.
3. Answers will vary. It's certainly not a call to stop enjoying entertainment (in which case, one would not read or watch movies of the Hunger Games trilogy. It may encourage readers to be more selective about their viewing, but many readers will focus on the love story or the war story rather than the invitation to rethink the entertainment industry.

Chapter 17, Training for the Capitol; Peeta at Dinner, page 48

1. Students' lists of reasons should include the following: Katniss's performance as the Mockingjay has succeeded in uniting the districts; she has not attended training sessions; she isn't good at taking orders; and she's not in peak physical condition.

2. Coin's response seems fair in that it addresses Katniss's lack of training, provides coaching in taking orders and an opportunity to improve her physical condition, after which, it seems, she will go through the standard approval process.

3. Possible response: Finding themselves in a similar position—provisionally unable to fight in the Capitol, which both are determined to do—they form an alliance that may improve both their chances of achieving their goals.

4. Answers will vary. Possible responses: If her doctors had offered it, or simply undertaken it, Johanna wouldn't have had a chance to steal Katniss's morphine, which set up an important conversation. If her doctors had offered it, she would have had no particular reason to interact with her trainer, giving us one less chance to see her passionate desire to get fight in the Capitol.

5. Possible response: Enhancing Katniss has been an important theme of the trilogy. She has been plucked, scrubbed, coifed, dressed, and made up for public presentation both as a tribute and as the Mockingjay. But the words used were always ordinary words: *embellish*, *enhance*, *alter*, etc. The word *sugarcoating* comes from the world of baking—one of the areas of Peeta's expertise and an area with which he still connects, as witnessed by his decoration of Finnick's and Annie's wedding cake. So it carries the suggestion of specifically making Katniss palatable, acceptable, and/or desirable to Peeta, the baker.

6. Possible response: One of Peeta's chief characteristics was a firm sense of who he was and what he wanted. It was his sense of self that allowed him (in contrast to Katniss) to realize how the Capitol was trying to control the tributes, and enunciate that he didn't want to be a piece in their games. It was also this well-defined sense that gave him the drive to plan and execute a variety of strategies to make sure Katniss survived the first Hunger Games she was in. That centered self and self-knowledge are both gone. Peeta's utterances are so different that it's hard to imagine them coming from the same consciousness, so much so that the suggestion that he is talking to himself as two different people makes a lot of sense.

7. Katniss achieves the best score in shooting with a gun in her class on her first day. By the end of the chapter, Johanna is firmly off morphling, Katniss's ribs are almost healed, and Johanna can assemble her rifle herself, earning them praise from their trainer, Sergeant York.

8. Possible response: If Gale took Katniss's comment seriously, you would think he would address it: after all, this is a critical self-esteem and self-knowledge issue. But if Gale had provided her with a fuller explanation, she would have felt better, and it would have been less of a problem, and there's still more than a third of the book to go with the relationships between Gale, Katniss, and Peeta to be worked out. So perhaps it wouldn't serve Collins's plan to have Katniss able to put that issue to rest at this point.

9. Answers should only include elements/situations that Johanna saw/experienced.

Chapter 18, The Star Squad; Peeta Joins the Star Squad, page 49

1. Plutarch suggests some propo shoots of Katniss and Peeta together, looking somewhat romantic. For the chief strategist of both the Games and the rebellion, Plutarch is strangely unaware of personal motivation: he has aimed wide of the mark in multiple conversations with Katniss, including when she sang the Hanging Tree and when he gave her guidance in the cavern during lockdown. Students may suggest that this dramatic lack raises the question of how he could engineer the Games and the response to the Mockingjay—both of which are rooted in psychology—with such a gap in his human understanding.

2. She realizes that—from the perspective of the military—her greatest failing is her inability to take orders.

3. At first she is excited to be with her friends and work under Boggs. She assumes the importance of the squad because they're in Command, although she realizes that it may have been a test. By the end of the chapter, she knows that the squad was put together to create propos, not to fight, as neither she, Gale, nor Finnick is ever chosen when a sharpshooter is needed. And when Peeta arrives to replace Leeg 2, Katniss realizes that the Star Squad has become a set-up to kill her.

4. Students should note similarities that lie in the existence of booby-traps; the intent to have them die in the arena; and the challenge of finding food and staying alive in an alien surrounding. They should identify disimilarities including that Snow is now a player in the games; that they have a gamemaker on their side, providing knowledge of some of the booby traps; that they are there as one squad in an invading army; that—as far as they know—the only person being personally targeted is Katniss, and that by their own side; that they came into the arena of their own choice; and that they have a goal other than to stay alive or keep another person alive (i.e., to kill Snow).

5. The bulk of the Capitol's air fleet was destroyed either during the invasion or in fighting in District 2, and if there are any left, they are probably being reserved as escape vehicles for Snow and his cronies. The invasion forces have been grounded because the Capitol's antiaircraft was doing too much damage as they attacked. Also, refraining from an air attack will keep the Capitol more intact, leading to less repair needed when the rebels take it.

6. Possible response: Yes. Turning the Mockingjay into an ordinary foot soldier would help dispel the clout and mystique attached to Katniss, rendering her less powerful, and allowing the new rebel government freedom from her influence. At the same time, if things go badly, they might want to bring her back, and having her and her costume available lays the groundwork for that eventuality.

7. Possible response: The Holo is a 3-D mapping device that "can neither send nor receive signals"—this means that it cannot receive (or send) updated information to overcome errors in its original programming, or (presumably) be tracked. It is voice-activated, and tied to both the squad commander and the voice of each squad member, the commander for most operations, but the entire squad for self-destruction should they or the Holo be captured.

8. Answers will vary. Plutarch's response efficient and characteristically devoid of insight. But since the replacement is Peeta and he's been assigned by Coin, it raises the question of whether Plutarch is part of the plot (if Katniss is right) to have her killed.

9. Answers will vary. Possible response: Coin's ultimatum to Katniss upon making the Mockingjay deal may have been a little extreme, but her response to Peeta's warning and Katniss's request to go to the Capitol to fight seem fair and reasonable, measured and deliberate. The only evidence that Coin has it in for Katniss is the fact that Peeta is there, but—if he's telling the truth about who sent him—it's strong evidence. It's not yet clear why Coin would be so desirous of getting rid of the Mockingjay, but some students may recall Katniss's thought in *CF* that she would be more valuable to the rebellion dead, as a martyr, while it would be better for the revolution to have Peeta alive (p. 244) and wonder if Coin has the same perception.

10. Student maps should include the Simulated Street Combat site, the workout site, Command, the hallway outside Command, Katniss's and Johanna's compartment; Mrs. Everdeen's and Prim's compartment; the woods outside; Johanna's room in the hospital; the shooting range; the area of the hospital where Mrs. Everdeen and Prim work; the hovercraft launch; the makeshift transportation area in District 12; the mountain tunnels leading to the Capitol; the rebel encampment inside the Capitol.

Test, Chapters 10–18, page 51

Vocabulary

1. These words are from the scene in Command when Katniss enters after passing her Block test in time to witness Plutarch's holograph demonstration.

2. These words are from the conversation between Plutarch and Katniss in which he refers to the attack on Peeta after he warns 13 of an attack as a "setback."

3. These words come from Katniss's reassessment of the role of the Mockingjay and the Star Squad three

days into their arrival at the Capitol.

4. These words name some of the content of the secrets Finnick revealed in the decoy propo aired while the victors were being rescued.

5. These words are related to the wedding of Finnick and Annie, and Plutarch's propo involving it.

6. These words name some of the tactics involved in the rescue of the victors.

7. These words are related to Katniss's injuries and treatment after Peeta attempts to strangle her.

8. These words relate to the Nut in District 2.

9. These words name three official causes of death of victims who were actually poisoned by Snow, and antidotes is how he was able to drink from the poisoned cup without dying.

10. These words occur in Katniss's recounting of what happens at the meal at which Peeta first joins the citizens of 13.

11. These are some of the weapons that were available in the old days—weapons that Plutarch wishes he had available.

12. These words have to do with the bunker in which Katniss and her family take shelter during the District 13 lockdown.

Essays

1. Possible response: If September 1 is the following week, then the day on which Katniss and Boggs discuss the date could be any day between August 19 and August 31. Students' estimates of time for the events reported prior to Chapter 11 should be reasonable and not contradict facts in the trilogy, and their explanations should provide rationales for the timeline they come up with.

2. Possible response: Yes, he knew. Evidence: To organize a rescue mission to the Capitol would have taken more than one day and would have had to be pre-planned. Haymitch has enough clout (demonstrated by his ability to convince Coin about the lockdown [with a little help from Katniss]; influence the direction of the propos, etc.) that he would have been in on it.

3. Possible response: In both cases, the Capitol is responsible for what Katniss brands as irretrievable. This shows that they have targeted her well, making her believe that there is no hope. Nevertheless, she runs after Prim, trying to find her, and she is not (so far) making similar efforts to try to recover Peeta. So perhaps, this perception is just what the Capitol wanted.

4. In *MJ*, Snow was evoked by his "gifts" of roses in Chapters 1 and 11 and appeared briefly in Chapter 9—Peeta's third and final interview. Katniss's propo in Chapter 8 is directed at him, and killing him was one (but only one) criterion for her to accept the role of the Mockingjay. Snow is also the focus of Finnick's revelations in Chapter 12, and the hand behind Peeta's torture. The subject of killing Snow first came up in *CF* as a distraction that Katniss made up for herself to stop thinking about the fact that she was going to kill her allies (p. 329). Some students may feel that these,, mainly indirect references are not enough to keep Snow placed as the arch villain, especially when—if Katniss is correct—Coin has just sent Peeta to kill her.

5. Students should recognize that this question harks back to Peeta's statement, "She has no idea. The effect she can have" (*HG* p. 91). This has been one of the key elements of Katniss's character—not realizing her attraction to Peeta and Gale; not realizing her influence as the Mockingjay. Students may either think that Boggs's statements in Command sifted into her consciousness, or that she's finally learning the skill of seeing how one is perceived, or that in order to create drama at this telling moment, Collins has made her realize in spite of her known limitations in this area for the sake of the plot.

6. Finnick's and Katniss's split announcement parallels two earlier interactions between Gale and Katniss, when one started "And may the odds" and the other completed ". . . be ever in your favor" (*HG* p. 8; *MJ* p. 128). The first time for Gale and Katniss, it was a sign of their solidarity. The second time, it seemed like Gale might not participate, and he does so only at the last moment. The I-have-your-back-and-you-have-mine closeness that Katniss once shared with Gale, she now shares with Finnick.

7. Students should include the following: The 74th and 75th Games were set up by the Capitol, with the 75th particularly designed to target victors. The 76th Games are an invasion of the Capitol by the rebels from all districts. The 74th and 75th Games only included Capitol citizens as prep team members, stylists, gamemakers, and other ancillary personnel (i.e., none were in the arena); the 76th Games are being played out on the streets of the Capitol with all Capitol citizens, including President Snow, facing the possibility of taking part. The 74th Games were restricted to children between the ages of 12 and 18; the 75th games to victors, the youngest of whom was 17 (Katniss). The 76th Games may involve people of any age (although there's no reference to Capitol children in the trilogy). In the 74th and 75th Games, the intention was that only one person survive. In the 76th Games, if one person—Snow—were to die and the rest surrendered, it's likely that everyone would be satisfied. In the 74th and 75th Games, there was limited ability to get

supplies into the arena from outside. In the 76th Games, the rebels from 13 are backed—and (we can assume) being supplied—by all the other districts.

8. It is ironic that the Capitol citizens—the only ones free from being sent to the Hunger Games arena and fighting to the death—live in an arena and may die simply by virtue of being in the Capitol.

9. In *HG*, the luxury train from 12 is met by excited crowds, anticipating the Games (Chapter 4). In *CF*, the arrival on the Victory Tour is passed over in Chapter 5; and the return as tributes is skipped over between Chapters 14 and 15. In *MJ* Chapter 18, a cargo car carries the soldiers from 13 into one of the tunnels under the mountains, and they hike into the Capitol from there on foot.

10. There are four assaults in Part II: the bombing assault on District 13; the rescue mission to free the victors held by the Capitol; the assault on the Nut in 2; and the beginning of the assault on the Capitol. Although the part title is singular (*assault*), it is possible that Collins is using it to refer to all of them.

11. As in other acts in the series, Act II of *MJ* may be said to have a double reversal: Katniss gets to the Capitol, despite all concerns that she might not make it; Peeta, who is likely to kill her, is sent to join her squad. It seems inevitable that both of these developments will drive the action of Part III, given its name.

12. Answers will vary, but could likely involve Katniss getting hold of a Holo and evading the squad (including Peeta); Katniss would try to figure out why Coin wants to kill her and how to "disarm" Peeta (for both their sakes); Boggs, whom Katniss has cast as a father figure, might do something to help her mission.

13. Possible response: If Katniss is correct, then first, readers should reexamine all of Coin's decisions and interactions with Katniss and second, it seems like Collins has purposely omitted to provide readers with some information about Coin.

14. Peeta is the odd man out in both the Career group and the Star Squad. In the first case, he had worked his way in with the Careers as a stratagem to keep Katniss alive by misleading them, which he did successfully up to a point, and then was wounded protecting her escape. In the second case, he is planted in a group (by Coin, it seems) for a purpose he is not even conscious of, which is directly contrary to his purpose when he was in control.

15. Answers will vary. Students may say that she has shown so little sympathy for Peeta that they would not be surprised if she killed him. They may also suggest that she'll try to evade the group or find another way to neutralize Peeta—anything to allow her to reach and kill Snow. Students who take the threat from Coin seriously may suggest that Katniss will at least consider targeting Coin or may pretend to take Peeta's explanation of his presence (to heat up the propos) at face value to see what develops.

16. In *CF*, the title of the last part ("The Enemy") may seem to readers to refer to different people at different times. The same thing may be true of the title of the last part of *MJ* ("The Assassin"): from the get-go, it could refer to Peeta (who has been programmed to kill Katniss); Katniss (who is hoping to assassinate Snow); and now possibly to Coin (who has set Peeta up to assassinate Katniss).

Chapter 19, "Real or Not Real?"; Boggs Steps on a Mine, page 52

1. Possible response: Coin is a power player who will let nothing stand in the way of her rise to power.

2. The closest parallel is her debt to Finnick for saving Peeta, which leads her to wonder how—being so much in his debt—she can now kill him in his sleep (*CF* p. 282).

3. Because Katniss has abandoned her promise to save Peeta and is treating him horribly.

4. She says her fixation with Snow "allowed" her to ignore the much more challenging problem of Peeta. Students may point out that this doesn't make sense and doesn't read as a true explanation of how she's behaved.

5. He says of his memory of Darius and Lavinia that "there was nothing . . . shiny about it" (*MJ* p. 274).

6. Students should see that it is distinguished by the detail in which she tells it, hinting that it is worthy of detailed attention.

7. Answers should only include elements/situations that Peeta saw/experienced.

Writer's Forum 4, Analyzing Nuance in Word Meanings, page 53

1. Students should note that star-crossed *lovers* (*HG*, p. 135) was the beginning of a charade; that Peeta suggested he and Katniss be *friends* (*CF* p. 51); that they became *affianced* as a strategy to satisfy Snow, not as the free choice of two people in love, as he would have wished, continuing their relationship's real/not real quality (*CF*, p. 73); that he and Katniss have each called the other a *mutt* (*MJ* pp. 190, 267); and that *ally* was notably used by Katniss to describe the beginning of developing a positive relationship with Johanna (*MJ* p. 235).

Chapter 20, Katniss Assumes Command; Peeta Asks for Death, page 54

1. Boggs says, "Don't trust them. Don't go back. Kill Peeta. Do what you came to do." Students should note that it is not clear if by *them*, Boggs means Coin and company or the rest of the squad. His directive not to go back could be both related to carrying out the mission and the repercussions of returning to Coin's control. Since he is convinced that Coin sent Peeta to kill Katniss, he is urging Katniss to protect herself by telling her to kill Peeta. And in his last sentence, he is giving his blessing for her operation, which he doesn't name, possibly for safety, in case anyone could hear him.

2. Homes administers first aid to Boggs and helps drag him inside. Finnick attempts to revive Messalla, warns the others about the black wave, and carries Messalla to the apartment. Boggs orders Katniss to get the Holo and transfers command to her. Jackson tries to communicate with the camp and orders a retreat. Gale and Leeg 1 minesweep, shoot open the lock on the building, and attempt to rescue Mitchell. Peeta grabs Katniss from behind and tries to smash her skull with his rifle and kicks Mitchell into a pod. Mitchell tries to subdue Peeta and is killed by the pod and the black wave. Castor and Pollux carry Peeta into the apartment. Katniss finds the Holo, accepts the transfer from Boggs, rolls out of the way of Peeta's attack, and helps finish bringing Boggs inside.

3. His situation has changed dramatically: previously he was unconscious of his programming and now, seeing his actions televised, he realizes his situation.

4. The Holo neither sends nor receives information, and an electromagnetic pulse device (Jackson surmises) has destroyed the field communicators.

5. Homes provides authoritative information in the form on an eyewitness account. Jackson implicitly relies on the military rules concerning chain of command. Katniss lies, invokes an authority that the others have no means of consulting to see whether her claim is accurate (President Coin's secret mission that only Boggs knew about). Katniss tells the truth about her mission, but couches it in terms that play to District 13's concern with having enough people to survive. Cressida also lies, adding Plutarch's authority and citing a logistical reason for Peeta's presence.

6. Having been declared dead, they can look forward to a period free from pursuit as they move toward President Snow. The people who will be hurt are their families and friends in 13 and elsewhere who see and believe the broadcast.

7. Boggs's death and transferring the Holo to Katniss give her one of the key things she was looking for. Successfully convincing the others gives her support and a guard for at least part of her mission. It's possible that either the squad will follow Peeta's suggestion and end that thread (which students may consider unlikely) or that Peeta's realization may either move him towards healing or make him worse: it's not possible to tell yet. Katniss could be hurt by concern about her mother's and Prim's (and Haymitch's) reactions to her death. Jackson's (grudging) willingness to help her with the Holo could pay off farther down the road as well. Others' commitment to her plan and willingness to lie for her may serve her: Capitol citizens' special knowledge of their community may turn out to be valuable.

Chapter 21, Two Farewells to Katniss; Underground, page 55

1. Persuasive techniques include appeal to law (Peeta saying he's guilty of murder); choice analysis (Finnick expressing why Peeta isn't culpable); putting oneself in other's shoes (Peeta seeing himself as others see him); logic (Peeta reasoning about the likely consequences of his continuing with them); appeal to rules and logic (Katniss referencing the mission that requires Peeta's participation).

2. Answers will vary. Students may say that the reference casts Peeta, again, as a lover, and this is an important shift in Katniss's feelings for him. Or they may say it isn't really appropriate because it calls up a romantic ideal of being joined in death to be free of the corrupt world—which doesn't reflect the situation. Some students may say that it would be more appropriate if Katniss recollected how she found a syringe and planned to kill Peeta when she thought they were captured by the Capitol at the end of *CF* (pp. 383–4).

3. Change in Peeta is shown by the return of his moral sensibilities and emotional engagement with the world; his giving Katniss the lamb stew, which has meaning from their shared past; his appeal to her for understanding of his situation; his insightful and kind comment to Pollux; his ability to categorize his recollections by whether they are shiny or not, to assist in discerning the truth; he doesn't recoil when Katniss touches him; he recognizes that she's trying to protect him. Changes in Katniss include her ability to consider Peeta as a victim of Snow, not just as a humiliation and threat to herself; her connecting Peeta to the lover in the song could herald a return of romantic feelings; her acknowledgment of battling for Peeta's survival, as well as her own; her gracious acceptance of the can of lamb stew; her acknowledgment that she can see Peeta's perspective; he appreciation of Peeta's comment to Pollux; her concern to be sure Peeta has eaten; her recollection of his shiny comment and interest in what he meant; her choice to stroke his hair; her "upgrading" their relationship from allies to "protecting each other" (even though the terms are synon-

ymous, the second is much warmer and more personal).

4. Possible response: Snow's farewell is an attempt to diminish the rebel cause, encourage the Capitol troops and Peacekeepers, and expose Katniss as a poor, misguided, incapable failure. Coin plays up the Mockingjay (no longer a threat to her power) as a slave who rose to lead a rebellion and whose memory is a continuing inspiration.

5. Peeta's wish for death was overcome with persuasion and a refusal to be moved by his desire for death. The squad's need for food was satisfied through Messalla's knowledge of where food stash's would be kept in this type of Capitol apartment. Katniss's inexperience with the Holo is partially overcome with Jackson's coaching. The decision of where to go next is arrived at by logic. The need to conceal their having been there is partially successful through locking a second bolt on the front door, straightening up, and hiding Castor's and Pollux's camera shells in a closet. Pollux's anxiety underground is at least partially quelled by Peeta's recognizing his value and (apparently) something to focus on.

Chapter 22, Lizard Muttations; A Kiss, page 56

1. Toward the end of *HG*, after Cato's death, when Katniss and Peeta go to the lake, he takes his knife out of his belt to drop it in the lake, but before he can let go, Katniss has an arrow aimed at his heart, thinking he poses a threat to her (p. 343).

2. Answers will vary. The text is unclear on the relationship between what Katniss says about his importance to the mission and how that weighs with Katniss's comment (p. 292) that she's battling for Peeta's survival as well as her own. Students may think that kissing him is the most manipulative thing she's ever done or a sign of how much she really cares for him.

3. Answers will vary. Students may mention: that Peeta is warning Katniss, not participating in the mutt attack; that the Peacekeepers find them so quickly; that the mutts decapitate the Peacekeepers; that Finnick dies. Astute students may raise the question of how it's possible—given the history—that there is no reaction from Gale to Katniss kissing Peeta and feel that Collins is using silence to avoid having to deal with the difficult love-triangle feelings at this point.

4. Students are likely to conclude that most of the choices are constrained—voluntary under the circumstances. The motivations for the soldiers probably include seeking a theoretical good of carrying out the mission, as well as the desire for life, liberty, and happiness, for the community. The squad is divided between those who know Katniss lied and those who don't, and Peeta, who is dealing more with his own issues than the squad mission. They all (again, excepting Peeta) know that she intends to kill Snow and are dedicated to helping her do that: Peeta is just trying not to do any more damage or fall into Snow's hands. For more than half the squad, their choice was final, because they're dead by the end of the chapter; for the others, its an ongoing choice.

5. Answers will vary. Students' endings should tie up loose plot ends and be in keeping with the material in the book thus far, and plausible in the world of Panem.

6. Grace periods that students mention should include *HG*: the quiet days during which Katniss recovers from tracker jacker venom and forms an alliance with Rue and the respite in the cave; *CF*: the last few days before the Quarter Quell, which Peeta and Katniss spend together and the time during which they hear Beetee describe his plan and undertake it; *MJ*: Finnick's and Annie's wedding and the time during which they're presumed dead. (There are other, shorter moments of interlude, as well.)

Strategy 9, Appreciating Genre Fusion, page 57

1. **War:** Collins leads up to the declared war in *MJ* with battle scenes that include the battleground, weaponry, tactics, strategy, and key personnel in *HG* and *CF* in the arenas, and clearly states the meaning of the conflict from the Capitol's view, while developing an alternative meaning to the rebels from what the Capitol intended. All three voumes include episodic battle descriptions, heroic action, and atrocities of war, and one of *MJ*'s focuses is the capture and treatment of prisoners. **Monster SciFi:** The mutts take us into the world of monster scifi: they are genetically engineered and designed to fight humans. Some are humanoid, like the mutts in the first arena, who have the tributes' eyes, and it could be argued that Katniss and Peeta both become monsterized humans. **Thriller:** Given that Katniss is in fear for her life for a large portion of the books, that Snow employs psychoogical warfare, that he is corrupt, that he is seeking to purposely undermine trust between districts and neighbors within districts, and that Katniss does not realize the full extent of the danger she is in, this fits the thriller genre well. **Action–Adventure:** Because the focus isn't simply on chases, guns, and bombs, but also ingenious solutions to challenging battle situations in exotic locations and an overarching quest, the trilogy also partakes of this genre. **Romance:** Although Peeta and Katniss go through some on-again-off-again, does-she-or-doesn't-she maneuvers, romantic love is on the

shelf for a lot of the trilogy while people are trying not to get killed, but the fact that the last discussion of the last chapter is about love and the epilogue includes babies (if not a happily ever after), entitles the trilogy to connection with the romantic genre.

Chapter 23, Refuge in the Fur Shop, page 58

1. The first is: "I know what blood poisoning is, Katniss . . . even if my mother isn't a healer."—repeated from *HG* p. 266 when Katniss is trying to conceal from Peeta how sick he is. The second is: " . . . you still have no idea. The effect you can have"—changed from third to second person and repeated from *HG* p. 91, when Peeta is trying to explain to Haymitch his perception of Katniss. The import is that he accurately recalls and appropriately uses some details from his shared past with Katniss without ill effect.

2. Katniss is focusing on the cost in human life, for which she thinks she is responsible; Gale is focusing on moving towards the mission's goal and serving the rebel cause.

3. Possible response: Students may think that there is nothing in Chapter 20 to support Cressida's interpretation of Jackson's perceptions: there is no reference anywhere to her implicit trust in Boggs, and she does not voice anything that explains her motivation.

4. According to Katniss, Plutarch's only concern is with the results of his spectacle, not with human life lost in the process.

5. Possible response: Peeta says, "They followed you because they believed you really could kill Snow," but if they did, it brings their training and ability to assess a mission into question, given that even with all the help she got, the strategy-savvy team members can't come up with a way to get access to him. In fact, she is only able to take a shot at him, because he is chained to a post and she is given an arrow by Coin's order, not because of the mission.

6. The parallel scene was Chapter 27 of *CF* (p. 390), in which Katniss has been blocking out the words of everyone, making them "meaningless and distant," until Gale, whom Katniss calls "someone I cannot block out," arrives and speaks to her. The change means that Peeta's influence on her now is stronger than Gale's.

7. Answers will vary. There are many reasons one might think one couldn't survive without another person: because one loved the person so much is one. For someone who has been compromised as much as Katniss, it might be someone who helps her through the bad times, during which he helps her see that life is worth living, as well as someone who understands what she's been through.

8. Answers will vary. Students may believe she will hatch another plan to kill Katniss, wait to see if Peeta finishes her off, or find a way to employ Katniss such that it appears that Katniss supports her.

9. Answers should only include elements/situations that Tigris saw/experienced.

Chapter 24, The Squad Splits Up; Gale Is Captured; Prim Dies, page 59

1. Student's should realize that Katniss's analysis is completely off base: she assumes things that are not implicit in Gale's words; her reasoning is convoluted ("can't survive without" ≠ "what my potential mates can offer me"); and his words do not necessarily imply an "unfeeling assessment." [Students may feel that Collins is forcing Katniss into a negative space by using her inability to interpret others. They may also point out that Katniss completely drops this train of thought in the morning (the following paragraph on p. 330) and never revisits it.]

2. Answers will vary. Students may interpret this to mean that the Capitol has now made mutts of their own citizens. Students may also question Cressida's use of present perfect tense, since Capitol citizens have demonstrated evidence of wildness prior to this (treating the violence of the Games as entertainment; going out of control when Peeta announced Katniss was pregnant—*CF* p. 256).

3. Short answer: it doesn't. Longer answer: Katniss and the others may have thought they would reach Snow's mansion and Cressida's prediction that he could help them navigate would be true; or it may have been a ploy to keep him alive.

4. An identical tactic for destroying people with bombs is described in the discussion of the new weapons Beetee and Gale are developing (*MJ* pp. 185–6): "Luring the victim into what appears to be a safe haven—where death awaits it . . . focused on . . . human impulses. Like compassion. A bomb explodes. Time is allowed for people to rush to the aid of the wounded. Then a second, more powerful bomb kills them as well."

5. It's not yet clear which side is responsible: the hovercraft bore the Capitol seal and the rebel medics weren't expecting the tactic because they rush to help the children. But the tactic is very specifically one that Gale and Beetee were known to be working on, and the Peacekeepers weren't expecting the attack either.

6. Answers should only include elements/situations that Gale saw/experienced.

Chapter 25, A Voiceless Fire Mutt; Meeting with Snow, page 60

1. First, "I am not pretty. I am not beautify. I am as radiant as the sun" (*HG* p. 121)—said when she sees herself in Cinna's interview dress. Second, "I look as if I have been coated in glowing embers—no, that I am a glowing ember straight from our fireplace" (*CF* p. 206). Here, in *MJ*, the two are combined: she is like the sun, and she is literally on fire.

2. Answers will vary. Possible response: She is being transformed—she assumes, by the Capitol—into a new form—which in her hallucinations, she perceives to be a fiery bird.

3. Possible response: She could burn to death, or, like the Phoenix (firebird) she could burn to the point of rebirth. She feels that she is currently doing neither.

4. If Katniss fires the last shot of the war in a spectacle featuring President Coin, it will be perceived that she supports the new regime (even if she doesn't say a word), which will presumably sway anyone who may not be wholeheartedly for Coin or who is looking to the Mockingjay for her take on the best future for Panem, thus serving Coin's ends.

5. A *mental Avox* is someone who has lost the power to speak through emotional, rather than physical, trauma. The cure suggested is to let Katniss be, and it works.

6. In Chapter 1, she said her name, age, district, that she was in the Hunger Games and escaped, and the rest focuses on Peeta being a prisoner, and that it's likely best if he is dead. In Chapter 25, she begins with the same three phrases, but then must alter because a) there is no longer a District 12 and b) she is in new circumstances (she's now taken down the Capitol) and her focus is now on revenge on Snow for killing Prim.

7. Possible response: Snow's argument that if he had a hovercraft, he would have used it to escape seems rational. His argument that he had no reason to kill the children or medics at that point is plausible: whether or not his statement that he was about to surrender was true, the rebels were at his gates; but, by making Snow appear to have killed a bunch of their children, the rebels had something to gain: the potential of destorying what was left of popular support for Snow. Snow's analysis of Coin's approach is upheld by the facts we've learned earlier, and even mirrors some remarks Katniss made about how 13 allowed the districts to be destroyed and didn't come to their aid (which Gale refuted at the time, *MJ* p. 28). Students may, however, point out that Snow is known to be a tactician who has been very careful to protect his power, proactively by murder if necessary, so it is extremely difficult to believe that he was so focused on a sixteen-yearl-old girl–however popular a celebrity she was—to the point that he ignored a seasoned and power hungry leader, like Coin.

8. He is referencing the supposed agreement he and Katniss made in *CF* Chapter 2 to tell each other the truth, which he clearly wasn't, since there is no way (and Katniss's recognizes this *CF* p. 71) that a teenager's love story could change the fury that she witnesses in districts 3, 4, and 8, and he must have known this.

9. Possible response: whether Katniss recovers her voice; whether Snow dies, and by whose hand; whether the Hunger Games are, in fact, over; what happens to all important characters: Katniss, Peeta, Gale, Mrs. Everdeen, Haymitch, Coin, Plutarch, Cressida, Pollux, including those we haven't heard about recently: Johanna, Enobaria, Effie Trinket, Annie; what happened to Madge and her family; why did Cinna choose District 12; why did Madge want so badly for Katniss to have the Mockingjay pin; does Katniss end up with Peeta (Gale seems pretty unlikely at this point).

Chapter 26, The Truth About Coin; The Vote; Assassination, page 61

1. Students may find that all of her arguments make sense except the emotional one that she herself refutes—that the rebels "wouldn't," and "couldn't" (p. 360) kill children and their own medics—and the suggestion that she is paranoid to consider that Coin would have targetted Prim to destroy Katniss.

2. She wants help working out who killed Prim, and she leaves after Haymitch makes a joke about advising Katniss about boys.

3. Students should recognize that Effie's presence is presented from the start of the trilogy as one of the key signals of a Hunger Games event. Because of her presence, we have the sense of the closing scene of the Games.

4. Possible response: If Katniss had not been reaped (presumably because Prim was not reaped) that particular year, she still might have seen and had to deal with the boy with the bread dying in the arena, and Gale wouldn still have passionate anger against the Capitol. It is unlikely that anything would have happened to convince her to change her mind and get married—more likely, Gale eventually would have

tried to join a rebel group somewhere. Certainly anything like a happily-ever-after ending with the Capitol still oppressing the districts seems highly unlikely. And they could never be outside the Capitol's reach, so talking about "without the Capitol's help" doesn't make any sense.

5. Possible response: This does not make sense: we know of no other weaponry experts in 13 besides Beetee and Gale. So if the rebels dropped the parachutes (and there's good reason to believe they did), whose parachutes would they be? We've been offered no alternative party who could take the blame. This seems to be Collins trying to have it both ways—blame the rebels, but not blame Gale. [Note: In the next chapter (p. 377), Katniss says definitively, "Coin thought the parachutes would expedite the war." This seems to settle the point that it was Gale's and Beetee's weapons that killed Prim, though Collins doesn't say so in so many words.]

6. Possible response: Peeta votes no because he's appalled at the idea of having any more Games. Johanna votes yes out of a desire for vengeance. Enobaria wants the Capitol citizens to experience being at the mercy of their own policies. Annie votes no because Finnick would have done so and because getting rid of the Games was part of the reason for the rebellion (agreeing with Peeta). Beetee votes no for logical and pragmatic reasons of survival. Katniss votes yes, using Prim as a reason, in order to make Coin think Katniss is on her side so she can carry out her assassination without suspicion. Haymitch votes yes because he understands what Katniss intends to do, and his choice of words —"I'm with the Mockingjay" (not "I'm with Coin")—make it clear that he understands what Katniss is thinking..

7. Answers will vary. Possible response: Katniss decided to kill Coin when she placed her vote: she never would have agreed to another Game. She voted to make Coin think she had Katniss's support and keep Coin from having suspicions about putting a weapon in Katniss's hands. Astute students may pose several objections to how Collins has handled this: 1) Katniss's seeming recollection that Snow and she had an agreement to tell the truth as she stands bow in hand also seems like a deciding moment. The existence of two deciding moments seems irreconcilable. 2) Katniss's believing that she and Snow have an agreement cannot be reconciled with her acknowledgement in *CF* that he made that supposed agreement while sending her on what he must have known to be an impossible mission (i.e., he said he was promising to tell the truth, even as he lied), and in this chapter (p. 360), her accurate assessment that Snow has always been manipulating her.

8. Answers will vary and should include students' assessments of Snow's, Coin's, Katniss's, Peeta's, Gale's, and Haymitch's intentions.

Strategy 10, Drawing on History and Mythology: Sparatcus and Theseus, page 62

1. Students' maps should show Thrace, Macedonia, Capua, South Italy, Alps, Strait of Mesina, Sicily, Cantenna; Crete, Athens. [Note that some of the places are named in proper adjectives, not just proper nouns.]

2. Collins said in an interview that Katniss follows the same trajectory as Spartacus, "from slave to gladiator to rebel to face of a war" ("Suzanne Collins's War Stories for Kids" April 8, 2011 *New York Times* http://www.nytimes.com/2011/04/10/magazine/mag-10collins-t.html?pagewanted=all&_r=0).

3. Katniss volunteers as a tribute to free one person (Prim); whereas Theseus intended from the start to end the custom. Katniss does end the custom when she shoots Coin. The arenas and the pod-laced streets and underground paths of the Capitol may be compared to labyrinths.

Chapter 27, Return to 12, page 63

1. Although it *seemed* upon seeing the Mockingjay suit's special pill pocket, accessible with just the teeth, that Cinna had thought of everything and provided a sure means for Katniss to commit suicide if she found herself in an untenable situation, he did not (and could not) foresee Peeta's intervention to save Katniss's life. Likely, this is why Collins chose to use the word *seems*, rather than saying "Cinna has thought of everything," which the events of Chapter 27 would have rendered untrue.

2. She decides to take her own life.

3. She insists he could see her on the screen, but that is far from meaning that he was in a position to take a shot, if he wished to. It's also possible that—having a better sense of what makes other people tick—he knew that suicide was not necessary.

4. Answers will vary. Possible response: Just as you once thought it would be best for Peeta if he were dead (*MJ* p. 4) and it turned out not to be true, so it is not best if you are dead, even though I don't think you can see it now.

5. She says that "taking my life is the Capitol's privilege. Again." but then describes herself to well on her way to starving herself to death when Haymitch comes to take her home. So it's not clear what, besides her freedom was really taken away.

6. Katniss's statement, "Coin thought the parachutes would expedite the war," (p. 377) leaves no doubt she now knows/believes that the rebels blew up the children and the medics.

7. Possible response: Katniss was not condemned due to the testimony of Plutarch, now secretary of communications, and Dr. Aurelius, who presented Katniss as a "hopeless, shell-shocked lunatic" (p. 378).

8. Students may tend to believe that Collins would agree. They may point out that Plutarch has been the one to make the broad political statements that reflect an appreciation of the American system of representative government (p. 83), and his role is to assess the big picture. Their own views will vary.

9. His first action is to plant primroses at Katniss's house in memory of Prim. It shows compassion, consideration, and an ability to act for Katniss when she cannot act for herself.

10. Students are likely to conclude that the title of Part III of *Mockingjay*, like Part II: "The Assault," and the last part of *HG* ("The Victor") and *CF* ("The Enemy") is meant to be read in multiple ways, in this case referring to: 1) Peeta as the intended assassin of Katniss; 2) Katniss, who intends to assassinate Snow (without a trial); 3) Katniss, who succeeds in assassinating Coin.

11. Students' drawings or titles should represent important material in each chapter.

Strategy 11, Identifying Themes in a Series, page 64

1. Possible responses: *MJ* repeats the themes of: Appearance vs. Reality ("Real or Not Real"; what is the truth about Coin?). It extrapolates the themes of: the Power of Partnerships by showing the importance of the Star Squad's various skills in moving them through the Capitol and in helping in Peeta's rehabilitation; Internal vs. External Identity in that Katniss has the chance to redefine herself after she is done being a piece in other people's games. It personalizes the theme of Desensitization to and Through Violence by showing the results of Gale's murderous anger in the death of Capitol children and rebel medics, including Prim. It deconstructs the theme of Bread and Circuses by demonstrating a real, celebratory (wedding) feast in 13, when the Capitol is having food shortages, in renouncing the Hunger Games, in the warped experience of Katniss who doesn't say she was shot, but that she saw herself shot on television, and in the choice to televise on-the-spot coverage of the war and of Katniss's trial. Food as Power is resurfaces in a twisted fashion in the imprisonment of Katniss's prep team for violating the strict distribution laws of District 13, which allowed it to survive.

2. Answers will vary. Students should support their position.

Writer's Forum 5, Comparing Treatments with Multiple Parts, page 65

1. Answers will vary. The movies are not yet out at this writing, but since Snow's granddaughter is in the movie of *CF*, it's a good guess she's going to figure in the movie of *Mockingjay* in ways that are not in the book (in which she never appears and her existence is only mentioned once by Johanna, p. 369), and since a good portion of the trailer looks like a war movie, it seems like that aspect may be emphasized. Students should use the film vocabulary in their film analysis.

2. Answers will vary. Students should use the vocabulary of literary analysis and film analysis to compare and contrast the book and film versions.

3. Answers will vary. Students may suggest that it may be more difficult to craft a unified vision with so many creators involved.

Writer's Forum 6, Writing an Epilogue, page 66

1. Now that the end of Chapter 27 has established that Katniss loves Peeta, readers may wonder if the dramatic changes in her life situation will change her attitude toward having children (*HG* p. 9), now that they are not in danger of being reaped.

Epilogue, Children; Explaining the Past, page 67

1. Twenty years (p. 390, next to last sentence).

2. Possible response: Because they are not named, they represent the entire new generation of Panem—the post-Hunger Games children. If they had been named, they would have just been two individuals.

3. They each have a mix of Katniss's dark hair and gray eyes and Peeta's blond hair and blue eyes: they are each clearly a combination of both their parents.

4. Possible response: It takes longer to say as written, and for that reason, gives more of a sense of passing time.

5. Answers will vary. Students may think that because Katniss characterizes her fear as being "as old as life itself," she may be referencing the fears that all mother's have for the child they are carrying and completely responsible for. Given her background, however, and history of knowing any child could be taken and

killed by the state, it would seem that some of her fear would be related to that.

6. Possible responses: The meaning of the song that Katniss sang to Prim and Rue is confirmed: it is possible for the world described by the song to be the real world in which we live, not just a dream that we wish reflected reality. | Music (and art) reflect what is best in people: our hightest aspirations, our care for each other.

7. It would seem to symbolize a kind of resurrection: they have—without knowing it—changed the meaning of the landscape from a killing field just by their presence, making it something fresh, innocent, and beautiful

8. The book of people that she, Peeta, and eventually Haymitch, put together, telling of all the people they loved and lost in the Hunger Games and the war.

9. Students may point out that the first use of *game* (in *Hunger Games*) is a euphemism and the second use is a stretch of the meaning of the word (Katniss's practice of thinking of acts of goodness to drive away despair), but the fact that the same word is used is meant to connect and tie up the end of the series neatly.

10. Answers will vary. Students may think it likely that Katniss will experience something much more akin to despair and depression, such as what took over her mother after her father's death or herself upon her return from the Capitol the last time, something far more seriously devastating to her well being than "not taking pleasure" in things. Students may also point out that if she were simplifying her description as if she were addressing her children, a simpler expression than "taking pleasure" (enjoy?) would be more appropriate. All-in-all, this seems to downplay Katniss's pain.

11. Answers will vary. Students may think it likely that Katniss also has memories of being unable to save people from terrible deaths, of people dying at her hands, of psychological torture, etc, that somehow she's passed over in this description.

12. Answers will vary. Students should support their stances.

Strategy 12, Analyzing the End of a Series, page 68

1. Possible response: Plutarch's commentary on the human race, which stands for Collins's take, makes it clear that the ending is equivocal: it's not really the end, and given our history, we could easily end up in a similar place again. Besides that, there is also a mix: many have died, but those who are alive have things to live for: children (Katniss, Peeta, Annie), better healthcare (Mrs. Everdeen), establishing a representative government (Plutarch), etc.

2. Possible response:
- Will Katniss kill President Snow? (If he died laughing because she shot Coin, then she sort of did.)
- Will the Hunger Games come to an end? (Yes.)
- What will Katniss do to Coin, who tried to have her killed and killed her sister? (Kill her.)
- Where will District 12 residents go if the war is won, since 12 is destroyed? (Back to rebuild 12)
- What happened to Madge and her family? (The same thing that happened to the rest of District 12: no special treatment for the Mayor.)
- What happened to Buttercup? (He went home and—seeing as Prim was gone—made peace with Katniss.

3. Annie, Mrs. Everdeen, Katniss and Peeta, Gale, Haymitch, Buttercup, Greasy Sae and her granddaughter.

4. Answers will vary. Possible response: Katniss is now a private citizen, living life with the freedom of individual choice that she longed to have in the beginning of the trilogy, and able to focus on her family, without responsibility for the entire country.

5. Possible responses: What happened to Tigris, the prep team, Effie, Johanna, and Enobaria after the war was over? Why did Cinna choose District 12?

6. Possible response: We know that President Snow knew about Katniss going to the woods, so Plutarch knew, too. As a secret member of the team planning a rebellion, he thought that Katniss, with her hunting skills and because she represented the district that everyone thought poorly of could be groomed to become the face of a rebellion. And he thought it would be even more effective if she volunteered rather than being chosen herself, so he made sure that Prim was chosen. The tracking cameras also led him to realize that Peeta was in love with her, so he had a unique opportunity to set up a situation where two tributes would be working to save one, and he could try to make sure she won, but without doing anything overt that President Snow would notice. He gave Cinna—part of the rebellion—a head's-up, and Cinna chooses 12 for this Hunger Games, letting other people think it's nothing more than the fact that he likes a challenge, and no one is suspicious.

Strategy 13, Understanding Tropes page 69

1. **Poison Immunity**: President Snow has an antidote (that only partially works), that allows him to poison enemies for years without being suspected. **Cult of Personality**: Through circumstance, chance, and deft behind-the-scenes planning and media action, Plutarch, Cinna, and Haymitch forge a teenage girl into the face of a rebellion. **Big Bad**: Snow is the original Big Bad, but he has competition from Coin at the end. **Archenemy**: Snow is the original Archenemy, but Coin gets in on this as well. **It's All My Fault**: Katniss suffers from this a lot. Snow helps convince her. **Outliving Usefulness**: Snow never really had a *use* for Katniss: he was just trying to use her for damage control. But Coin did have a use for her, and then wanted her gone. **I Work Alone**: Katniss tries this in the Quarter Quell and aims to try it in the Capitol. She does better with allies. **Terrorist or Freedom Fighters**: It's arguable that Katniss is a freedom fighter and Gale is a terrorist. **Gladiator Revolt:** The districts are slaves of the Capitol: the arena is similar to gladiatorial combat; the victors form a key part of the Star Squad.

Test, Chapters 19–27, page 70

Vocabulary

1. These words relate to Katniss's imprisonment after shooting Coin.
2. These words relate to Katniss's and Gale's progress through the streets of the Capitol after leaving Tigris's shop, up until Gale's capture.
3. These words have to do with the means by which the Star Squad moved underground from the apartment.
4. These words relate to Katniss's unintentional visit to President Snow in captivity in the mansion.
5. These words relate to Tigris and her fur underwear shop.
6. These words relate to Coin's on-air presentation about Katniss after her supposed death.
7. These words related to the bombing of the children and Katniss being set afire.
8. These words describe the appearance and actions of the lizard mutts that chase the Star Squad.
9. These words are part of Plutarch's description of human beings.
10. These words relate to Katniss's first days and weeks back in District 12.
11. These words relate to what the Star Squad faced immediately after Boggs stepped on the bomb.

Essays

1. She might have thought of her time on the hovercraft when she was having the same concerns, and stole a syringe with the intention of killing him to keep him from being tortured or killed by Snow. (*CF* p. 383)
2. Answers should include the name *Primrose*, the use of roses in presenting the star-crossed lovers, the rose that Snow always wears, Snow's use of roses to terrorize Katniss at home, in District 13, and in the Capitol, Katniss's choice of a rose for Snow's execution, and Katniss's meeting with Snow in his greenhouse.
3. 74th Hunger Games: Katniss uses tracker jackers to dispel the Careers (and Peeta) camped beneath her tree. They are all stung and several die. Wolf muttations with the eyes of tributes chase the three remaining tributes near the end of the Games, give Peeta the bite that leads to his leg being amputated, and torture Cato until Katniss kills him to release his suffering. 75th Hunger Games: There are several types of mutts in the arena, each in its own sector: the orange monkey mutts that kill the District 6 morphling, the insects, the jabberjays that sound like loved ones—which target Katniss and Finnick and lead to the revelation that everyone Johanna loved had been killed, and the never-clearly-identified beast that rips tributes to pieces. 76th Hunger Games/War: Lizard mutts chase the Star Squad underground, reeking of roses, hissing Katniss's name, and decapitating anyone in their path, including Peacekeepers, and Jackson and Leeg 1, and Finnick, Homes, and Castor. Johanna identifies Peeta's after his rescue as the "evil-mutt version of " himself (*MJ* p. 243), the intended result of which is the murder of Katniss, and Katniss identifies herself as a fire mutt, which contributes to her suicide attempt.
4. In *HG*, Peeta warned Katniss to run when she was collecting the bow after the tracker jacker attack, and he realized—but she didn't—that Cato was bearing down on them (p. 193). In *CF*, Peeta warns Katniss to run when he sees that Gale is being whipped in the Town Square and is afraid Katniss will either a) be targetted if she shows her face or b) will do something stupid (p. 104). In *MJ*, there are two warnings: first, in his last interview, when Peeta warns of the attack on District 13 (p. 133); second, Peeta is stirred from sleep by the hissing of the lizard mutts and warns Katniss (pp. 304–5). The parallels show that—no matter when or where or what condition he's in, Peeta is always looking out for Katniss's well-being.
5. Students should recognize these key points. Music is Katniss's heritage from her father, and her ability to make birds go silent is a sign of the quality of her voice. Peeta fell in love with her listening to her sing. Music gives Katniss a way to interpret difficult situations (references to "The Hanging Tree" to express her

desire to have Peeta dead rather than tortured); it shows the ideal of what life could be like (the lullaby sung to Prim and reiterated in the Epilogue); it is a comfort to the dying (Rue); and a restorative force (during her imprisonment awaiting her trial, though she still intends to die and stops singing when she gets home, as far as we know—so this is hard to construe).

6. Possible response: Yes: since they never had a good relationship, what they have in common is Prim, and her loss leads them to give up their old prejudices and befriend each other. In a safe environment with enough to eat, Katniss can afford to be generous with her love and her bacon, unlike when she first met Buttercup. The fact that he guarded Prim and traveled all the way from 13 trying to find her make him special in a way that no other creature can ever be. Katniss and Buttercup were alike in their acerbic, loner approach: their new harmony signals a new phase in Katniss's interactions with others.

7. She is referring to the rose that President Snow left for her, which is still inside the house.

8. Possible response: No. She has become a private citizen and will not seek publicity or celebrity again.

9. Answers will vary depending on the dystopia chosen for comparison.

10. Students should reccognize that the word *rebirth* (p. 388) connects with Katniss's description of herself on fire, which makes her sound like a phoenix (a bird that is consumed by fire and reborn from the ashes, p. 348), the reference to *metamorphosis* (p. 363), which is not as peaceful, as Katniss imagined it would be, and the graveyard that become a playground (p. 390).

11. Possible response: It is intended to signal the last shot of the war. Katniss makes it the last shot of the Hunger Games *and* the war.

12. Peeta says that murdering the innocent costs everything you are, but Katniss says that she has found in Peeta "the promise that life can go on, no matter how bad our losses. That it can be good again" (p. 388). Students may think that these two takes are contradictory or that Peeta was still in captivity and may not have realized what was possible or was making a rhetorical point.

13. Students should see that Plutarch is contradictory: he has insight and vision for peace, but he is a Gamemaker; he can see the big picture, but doesn't understand the emotions of individuals; he may have been party to sending Prim to the Capitol, although she was underage. Perhaps the rebellion wouldn't have happened had he not become a Gamemaker, though.

14. The phrase is the very one she found so offensive when Gale used it (p. 329), and the fact that she repeats it suggests that what she had said about Gale knowing her best was—at least sometimes—true (the rest of the time, it's Peeta who has the greatest insight into Katniss).

15. The climax is Katniss shooting Coin (and thereby killing Snow, if you read it that way).

16. Students should support their analysis with details. Possible response: cliff hangers: 1, 4, 8, 10, 11, 14, 21, 25; shockers: 3, 5, 9, 12, 15, 16, 18, 19, 20, 22, 24, 26; other 2, 6, 7, 13, 17, 23, 27, Epilogue.

Theme Page, page 73

Hero vs. Protagonist

1. Possible response: Katniss is a protagonist, not a hero. Peeta is at least heroic. I don't worship celebrities like they do, and I know it takes more than one person to save a country.

2. Possible response: Panem only needed a hero because of the corruption and oppression. In their current phase, they don't need one, but if the cycle starts again, as Plutarch suggests it may, the need may return.

Promises

1. Possible response: As the Choice Analysis Tool shows, hardly any choices (or promises) were made freely. Nevertheless, Haymitch, for example, tries to keep his promises, in as much as his drinking allows.

Lies

1. Possible response: No—Collins's characters are more complex than this, Haymitch, for example.

2. He promised Peeta to save Katniss; he promised Katniss to save Peeta; he planned to save them both.

Forgiveness

1. Possible response: Katniss and Peeta forgive each other in *CF* (p. 51), as do Johanna and Katniss in *MJ* (p. 235), and Katniss and Buttercup (pp. 386–7). Katniss can neither forgive Gale (p. 367) nor forget Prim's death. Students are likely to think that Beecher's advice is unrealistic.

Real or Not Real

1. Students should note that citizens are forced to conceal thoughts, tributes are forced into belying themselves, *games* and *peacekeepers* are some of the euphemisms, many people are trying to keep secrets.

Resurrection

1. Students should mention the bread that saves the starving family, Peeta coming out of his riverside grave, Peeta being brought back from the dead twice, and Katniss's personal resurrection through Peeta. The word *rebirth*, the firebird/phoenix imagery, and the reference to metamorphosis also tie to resurrection.

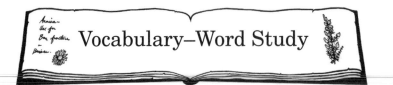

Vocabulary–Word Study

Using the Vocabulary–Word Study Feature

In keeping with the emphasis that the Common Core State Standards places on vocabulary acquisition and use, this section provides ideas for a variety of word study activities for preteaching vocabulary, drawing on the more than 2500 vocabulary words identified in the Hunger Games trilogy teaching guides. These activities also provide opportunities to teach or review a variety of topics including spelling rules, word roots and affixes, SAT vocabulary, multiple meaning words, shades of meaning, etc. You may wish to specify particular references for student, or you can allow them to choose dictionaries and thesauruses and encourage them to compare and contrast definitions, pronunciations, and even etymologies. Of course, you can also create your own word sets and activities. The entire list can be found on the Garlic Press website at http://www.garlicpress.com/resources ???

SAT and ACT Words

Collins uses a number of words or forms of words that typically show up on the SAT and ACT tests, so teaching this vocabulary can do double duty. There are not enough words in this list to create a lot of strong patterns, but students can define the words, identify the etymologies and pronunciations, and categorize the words by POS and/or origins, followed by using them in sentences.

accessible	concise	gingerly	judicious	precariously	scrupulously
acrid	congenial	hampered	lethargy	predators	scrutinizing
acutely	copious	illusion	levity	proximity	speculate
alleviate	delectable	impassive	linger	quell	stealthily
aloof	delusions	imprudent	malice	rambles	superficial
amiable	din	incident	meandering	rant	tentatively
arrogance	discrepancies	inconsequential	meticulous	recount	terse
aspire	disdainful	indifferent	mollified	remotely	thrive
attributes	dissonant	indignation	obscure obsolete	resolve	unprecedented
banal	eulogy	innovative	palatable	respite	vaporized
capricious	fervently	intimate	palpable	retrospect	vigilant
clandestine	frugal	intimidate	petty	savory	wary
complementary	furtive	irrefutable			

Jargon

Though the word *jargon* is sometimes used to refer to words that are meant to obfuscate, it is usefully applied to the specialized technical vocabulary of a field of study or endeavor, and this is how it is used here. Collins draws the most jargon, from four areas: hunting; fighting, tactics, and military activity; video production; and medicine, health, and human anatomy. Note that while video production vocabulary is almost entirely confined to *MJ*, the other jargon is more spread across the trilogy.

Vocabulary from each of these areas can be taught as a content-area set, and it is possible to add lower-level words from the books to help fill out the group. For example, there are a number of simple words having to do with the body, like shoulder, teeth, tongue, neck, head, and knee, which all appear in The Hunger Games. Word webs and Venn diagrams are useful for showing the relationships between and among words. Brainstorming categories —based both on content area categories (such as parts of the body and states of being) and on language criteria (such as words with the same POS, language of origin, root word, or synonyms)—and identifying which words fit the category, as well as adding words not found in the trilogy to each category are also worthwhile exercises. The number of words also allows for incorporating groups of them in short written or spoken pieces.

Other approaches could include using to label provided images (particularly for the body and medical equipment); or creating an image with labels. For words that share a root (conscious, consciousness), students could define one word in terms of the other.

Hunting

archery	carrion	game	predators	rabid	venomous
blind	decoy	gamey	prey	scavengers	vermin
carcass	entrails	notch	quarry	sheath	yearling
carnivorous	forage	poaching	quiver	venison	

Medicine, Health, and the Human Body

abdomen	conscious	fatigue	knocked up	psychological twist	socket
addictive	consciousness	fetal position	lethargy	puke	spinal cord
adrenaline	contagion	fixation	lunatics	pulse	stimulant
airway	contagious disease	gag reflex	maimed	pupils	strawberry birth-
amputate	contracted	gaunt	malnourished	quarantine	mark
anatomy	convalescence	gene pool	mangled	queasy	stupor
anesthetize	convulses	genetic code	marred	rabid	surgically
antidotes	debilitating	genetic diversity	marrow	radiation	sutures
antiseptic	delusional	genetically	medicinal	reconstructed	syringe
aorta	delusions	hacking	medics	recovery	tailbone
apothecary	depression	hallucinations	mental clarity	recuperating	tattoos
arteries	deprivation	herbalist	mentally disoriented	remedies	temporary insanity
asphyxiation	deranged	hormones	motor coordination	retch	tinctures
balm	detoxify	hyperventilating	noxious	retinal	tourniquet
bile	digestion	hypodermic needle	nutrition	rubbing alcohol	toxic
bowels	DNA	hysteria	ointment	salve	toxicity
catatonic	drip	hysterically	opiates	sanity	veins
chamomile	drug-induced	implantation	orifices	sedated	vials
cold collar	embryos	incapacitated	outbreak	edative	viruses
cold turkey	epidemic	infertile	paralyzed	semiconsciousness	vital signs
coma	excruciating	insane	paranoia	skeletal	windpipe
concussion	exhalations	intimate places	parched	sober	withdrawal
confined to bed	famished	intoxicated	posture	sobriety	wooozy

Video Production

airtime	camera-ready	dissemination	montage	replaying	spontaneity	superimposed
booth	camera ready	in reruns	off camera	right on cue	stage fright	televised
broadcast battle	cut	intercom	on cue	scripted	staged-looking	underscored
	cutting … together	intercut	on-camera talent	smash cut	studio approach	unscripted
	depiction	monitor	propaganda	sound stage	studio clips	wrap

Military, Tactics, Law Enforcement, War, and Fighting

ambush	cease fire	disinformation	garrote	minesweeping	security clearance
antiaircraft	cell disintegrator	electromagnetic	garroting	moppping up	soldierly
armored vehicles	combative	pulse device	hangar	mows down	solitary confinement
armory	coordinates	encampment	holographic image	national security	squadron
arsenal	corpse	evacuation	hovercraft	no-man's-land	stockades
assailants	corpse-littered	execution	human shield	nuclear develop-	stocks
assault	counterattack	fatalities	impenetrable	ment	switchblades
automatic weapons	counterstrike	firestorm	incendiary	nuclear war	traitor
ballistic	coup	flogging	incinerated	nuclear weapons	traitorous
barrracks	decapitated	foot soldier	incineration	nukes	treason
biological weapons	decimated	fortifications	infiltrated	overthrow	tribunal
blank cartridge	defection	fortified	knockout gas	rebel base	uprising
blowgun	demotion	fortress	lockdown	retaliate	vengeance
bludgeon	deserting	freedom fighter	militaristic	retaliation	vengeful
bunker	detonate	front line	militarized	revenge	weaponry
casualties	detonation	gallows	minefield	satellites	whipping post

Affixes and Roots

Knowledge of word etymology and word context are two key aids for inferring the meaning of unknown words. With so m vocabulary, we have a rich source that can be plumbed in different ways. For example, you could collect words: with an affix that has a single etymology; with an affix that has a single spelling but more than one possible source; that are the same POS but have different suffixes, and so on. For each words group, students can identify language of origin, define the word, identify its POS and pronunciation, identify other word parts and any spelling changes, and categorize words in various ways.

Here are some sets, starting with the three suffixes -ic, -ion, and -ible/-able. The words are presented in alphabetical order, so students can explore how the endings are added and, if you wish, (re)discover that, for example, -ion may actually be added as -ion, -sion, -tion, or -ation or try to discern rules for when to use -ible vs. -able.

-ion
aberration
absorption
accusation
acquisition
admiration
adoration
affectations
agitation
passion
allegations
alterations
altercations
annihilation
ascension
asphyxiation
extension
cessation
precision
commotion
compassion
concession
concoction
concussion
conditioning
configuration
confrontation
congestion
consolation
consternation
consumption
contagion
contortions
contraption
deceleration
deception
decomposition
defection
dehydration
delusional
delusions
demotion
depiction
depression
deprivation

detection
deterioration
detonation
devotion
digestion
discretion
disinformation
disorientation
disproportionate
disruption
dissection
dissemination
diversion
distraction
elation
electrocution
eruption
estimation
evacuation
exasperation
exceptional
execution
exertion
exhalations
exhibition
exoneration
expectations
extension
fixation
flotation
formation
fortifications
foundations
functional
fusion
hallucinations
illumination
illusion
immersion
implantation
implication
incarnations
incineration
indentations

indignation
indiscretion
infractions
installations
intentionally
interaction
interrogation
intersection
intervention
justification
limitations
malfunctioned
migration
motivational
national
nutrition
oblivion
oppression
orientation
penetration
perceptions
precaution
projection
proposition
provisions
provocation
purification
radiation
rational
realization
rebellion
reception
recognition
reconciliation
recreational
recrimination
reflection
regulation
rehabilitation
rendition
repercussions
replication
reposition
reservations

resolution
retaliation
retribution
revelation
revulsion
salvation
sanctioned
seclusion
socialization
speculation
transformation
transgression
transition
validation
variation
ventilation
vibration

-ic
aerodynamics
anticlimactic
antics
antiseptic
astronomical
authenticity
automatic weapons
being ironic
biological
catatonic
caustic
caustically
claustrophobic
dynamic
eccentric
ecstatically
emphatically
enigmatic
epidemic
erratic
exotic
genetic
genetically
go ballistic
histrionics
holographic image

hypodermic needle
hysterically luna-
   tics
maniacally
melodic
militaristic
mimics
pathetic
prophetic
psychological twist
public
republic
robotic
sadistic
spastic
static
stoically
strategically
surgically
symmetrical
sympathetic
synthetic
tactic
technically
technological ex-
   pertise
that's optimistic
theoretically
toxic
toxicity

-ble
acceptable
xsaccessible
accountable
amiable
audible
dabbles
desirable
despicable
discernible
disposable
double
durable
edible

expendable
impassable
impenetrable
imperceptible
improbable
inaccessible
incalculable
incorruptible
indelible
indistingushable
individisble
inescapable
inevitable
inexcusable
inexplicable
inseparable
insurmountable
invaluable
invincible
irrefutable
inseparable
irretrievable
irreversible
palatable
palpable
plausible
salvageable
sociable
sustainable
unacceptable
unbearable
undeniable
undetectable
unendurable
unfathomable
unforgettable
unintelligible
unpredictable
unquenchable
unstable
unsustainables
unthinkable
untouchable
vulnerable

Suffixes and Inflectional Endings

Here are some groups of words for suffixes that are less often seen. Of course, you can use the list to create groups for more common suffixes, such as -s, -ed, -ing, -er, -est, -ly, -ment, -ant/-ent, -ance/-ence, -ous/-ious/-eous, etc.

-ia
claustrophobia
cornucopia
hysteria
paranoia

-some
gruesome
loathsome
worrisome

-ism
barbarism
cannibalism
optimism

-ity
atrocity
authenticity
legality

-ency
consistency
despondency
leniency
proficiency
urgency

-age from French
camouflage
entourages
masssage

People Who Do Things

Though this is a small group, it exhibits a variety of endings for people's jobs, roles, and characteristics.

apothecary	captors	herbalist	insiders	law enforcers	oppressors	sharpshooters	stylist
beauticians	colleagues	immigrants	instigator	lunatics	racketeers	sniper	survivor
breeders	escort	inhabitants	lackey	mentor	savages	stonecutters	traitor

Prefixes

Anti- and *syn-* are less often seen, but each has four examples in our list, and *-syn* is good for introducing a discussion of assimilation, which you can then extend to *ad-*, *com-*, *-in*, *-ob*, and *-sub*. Of course, you can use the list to create groups for other common prefixes, such as *un-*, *under-*, *pre-*, *pro-* from Latin, *re-*, *dis-*, *en-*, and *ex-*, and also find one example each for *hyper-*, *hypo-*, *para-*, and the Greek *pro-*.

Homonyms/Multiple Meaning Words

There are many multiple meanings words and homonyms in the trilogy, but not all are in the same form. Each teaching guide uses "MM" to show pairs within a volume. When the usage is in multiple books, you can use the list below., which includes definitions and page numbers, using Roman type for *HG*, italic for *CF*, and bold for *MJ*. Students can identify the POS, pronunciation, and etymology for each word, as well as determine relationships and use them in writing or speaking, perhaps using the various meanings in a single sentence.

backfired 63 had a harmless explosion in the exhaust system
backfiring 91 having the reverse effect of what was intended
bolt 86 move suddenly and swiftly
bolt 103 fasten w/ a bolt; lock
bound 42 placed in a cover for protection
bound 55 likely
bounties 327 rewards
bounty 149 many items, supplied at no cost
conscious 147 aware
conscious 11 no longer unconscious; awake and aware
dart 308 glance
darts 199 small, pointed missiles shot from a blowgun
derailed 149 halted; stopped
derailed 132 having been knocked off the tracks
down 48 soft, short hairs
down 295 goose feathers
fend (for) 188 provide for
fend (off) 19 avoid; ward off
fuse 341 combine
fuse 256 material along which a flame moves to explode a bomb,
  allowing the bomber time to escape
grazed 312 scraped the skin, w/ little or no bleeding
grazing 54 feeding on grasses and other plants at their leisure
  in a pasture
greenery 34 green parts of plants—leaves, stems, etc.
greenery 166 plant greens used for decoration
gritty 61 having small, rough particles
gritty 28 abrasive; harsh
hacking 151 chopping w/ sharp blades and heavy, irregular
  blows
hacking 208 coughing harshly in spasms
haze 72 confused state of mind
haze 89 air clouded by smoke or particles
jerk 27 pull sharply
jerk 28 obnoxious or contemptible person
manning 370 being in charge of
manning 209 operating
merciful 162 kind; humane

mercifully 41 to my great relief
muted 34 (of sound) diminished
muted 353 (of color) not bright
obliged 327 required
obliging 211 willing to work w/ others
obscure 93 hide
obscure 300 hidden; not easy to discover
plunk 315 sit down heavily
plunking 158 dropping w/out trying to be gentle
quarry 119 hunted animals; prey
quarry 193 deep pit from which stone is dug
quiver 101 a case to hold arrows
quiver 282 slightest movement
radiating 268 extending in straight lines from a center
radiating 124 being emitted from
radiating 156 reflecting heat back
refuse 17 say no to
refuse 9 garbage
resonate 113 evoke a shared feeling
resonates 146 is filled with an echoing sound
shaft 70 body of an arrow - the straight stick
shafts 174 rays
shafts 207 tubes for carrying a substance (e.g., air)
sheath 5 case that is open at one end
sheath 166 close-fitting dress w/ a narrow, tapered skirt
spasm 33 sudden, involuntary muscle contraction
spasms 133 sudden, brief spells of emotion
stalk 92 to walk with strong, angry steps
stalking 155 pursuing as prey
sustained 322 received; suffered
sustaining 281 keeping up; continuing
tread 288 footsteps
treads 298 strips of material to help prevent slipping
unraveled 359 made clear
unraveling 56 untying
wedge 219 squeeze
wedge 268 shaped like a slice of pie

Synonyms: Distinguish Nuances and Connotations

Collins uses a number of word sets with closely related meaanings, providing an opportunity for students to make distinctions. Students could start by defining each word and identifying its part of speech, denotation(s), and connotation(s), and then go on to make distinctions between the synonyms. Alternatively they could define one word and define the other words in terms of the first defintion. Note that the part of speech of some of these words have been altered from Collins' use to create sets that have the same POS, and will thus be easier to work with for distinguishing nuances.

swerve / veer
groggy / woozy
armory / arsenal
contempt / disdain
alcove / nook
cunning / wily
welt / weal
snout/muzzle
hinder / curb
deplete / diminish
absolve / reprieve
clots / congeals
tailspin / nose dive
scuttle / slither
muffle / mute
distract / divert
impulse / whim
sprawl / splay
quench / stifle
drift off / slumber
evade / obscure
retch / puke
curt / terse
tad / token
frail / vulnerable
flinch / wince
woozy / groggy
toxic / noxious
aghast / appalled

abundance / bounty
populace / inhabitants
coil / reel / cylinder
casualties / fatalities
immunity /resistance
forbearance / patience
acerbic / caustic / snarky
scorching / searing
transfixed / stunned
demoralized / dispirited
slog / trudge / trek / tromp
flagrant / flamboyant
muddle / mishmash
provoked / smoldering
endangered / in jeopardy
debris / ruins / wreckage
ointment / salve
impulsive / capricious
abate / diminish / alleviate
brutal / inhuman / brutish
putrid / decomposing
immerse / submerge
carcass / corpse / carrion
menacing / ominous / sinister
copious / voluminous
traitorous / back-stabbing
unforeseen / unanticipated
delusion / hallucination
cast ... off / drove ... away
metamorphosis / rebirth

embellishments / enhancements / alterations / supplements
foil / counteract / avert / prevent
abhorrent / loathsome / despicable / repellent / odious
feral / savage / brutal / vicious
maimed / incapacitated / mangled / disfigured / marred / ravaged / wracked
counterattack / counterstrike / retaliation
retaliation / revenge / vengeance
contemplating / mulling over
bedraggled / disheveled / unkempt / scruffy
unnerved / distraught / disconcerted / disgruntled / ruffled
encased / encompassed / engulfed / immersed
delirious / exhilarated / giddy
stealthy / furtive / clandestine / covert
baffled / befuddled / disoriented / mentally disoriented
fury / homicidal rage / indignation / outrage
hazardous / perilous / precarious
vaporized / disintegrated / obliterated / incinerated
commotion / din / bombardment / ruckus
stupor / semiconsciousness / catatonic / coma / haze/ oblivion
deception / subterfuge / hoax / decoy / diversion
steel (oneself) / brace (oneself)
luscious / delectable / succulent
decadent / sumptuous / extravagant / plush /upscale
tainted / putrid / decomposing
temporary insanity / meltdown
incomprehensible / unfathomable / unintelligible / garbled
uncomprehending / slow on the uptake / dense
terminated / adjourned / revoked / annulled / repudiated
adjacent / adjoining / verging

Phrasal Verbs

Phrasal verbs are those verbs that include a particle. Particles in phrasal verbs look like prepositions or adverbs (or both), but they have a different function. Some verbs are characteristically followed by a prepositional phrase, and those that require an object may rarely or never appear without one. But a phrasal verb is different: if you take away the particle(s), the main verb means something completely different. Here's an example:

Verb followed by preposition: I don't like to *go under* the water.

Phrasal verb: The business is doing so poorly, it's about to *go under*.

In the first phrase, you could substitute another phrase, like "beneath the water" or "into the water." But you cannot make this type os substitution in the second case because *go under* is a single unit.

There are some of each construction in the vocabulary list: sometimes a preposition or adverb follows a verb in order to make it easier to define. Here is a list of the phrasal verbs only. Students can define them, compare them with other phrasal verbs that use the same verb or particle, or with the meaning of the verb without a particle.

out	broken in	caving in	clock out	drift off	mopping up	rat out	ticks off
break in	broken out	chugging back	clocked in	flipping out	mows down	sleep in	warding off
break into	cast off	clear with	cutting together	holding out on	open up	sleep off	weights on
breaks down	cater to	clinch it	decks out	knock(ed) up	ramp up	take out (kill)	whip up
broken down							

Compound Words

In this section, we have vocabulary words that are one of the three types of compounds: open, closed, or hyphenated. Phrasal verbs are not included in this listing, nor are idiomatic phrases.

Open

Open compounds often come from a modifier-noun combination that proves so useful, it becomes "set" as a phrase. But other relationships are possible, e.g. in *law enforcers*, which means "enforcers of the law," which is a shortened prepositional phrase, and students could identify the relationship, as well as word meaning and POS.

acceptable risks	contagious disease	gag reflex	metal detectors	power plays	split end
architectural design	criminal activity	garment bag	mixed bag	pruning shears	stage fright
automatic weapons	death warrant	gene pool	moot point	psychological twist	standard of living
barbed wire	double deal	genetic code	motor coordination	public eye (the)	strawberry birth- mark
biological weapons	double take	genetic diversity	mutual under- standing	rabbit warren	supply chain
black market	double vision	good form	national security	rag doll	temporary insanity
blank cartridge	dust motes	grace period	nick of time	rallying point	tiger lily
breeding stock	electromagnetic pulse device	gut feeling	nuclear develop- ment	rebel base	tracker anklet
brute force	emotional trauma	handheld commu- nicator	nuclear war	redeeming quality	tree line
camera ready	expiration dates	holographic image	nuclear weapons	rubbing alcohol	vantage point
cell disintegrators	fashion accessory	homicidal rage	obstacle course	security clearance	virtual tour
centralized govern- ment	fashon statement	human shield	patchwork quilt	shock waves	vital signs
clockwork precision	fetal position	hypodermic needle	piece of work	slag heap	water purification
cold collar	flat out	knockout gas	point of reference	solar batteries	whipping post
cold turkey	foot soldier	last resort	power failure	solar energy	
collective thinking	freedom fighter	laughing stock	power player	solitary confine- ment	
	front line	law enforcers		spinal cord	

Closed

Characteristically, oft-used open compounds tend to become closed, so it could be interesting to try to work out the word history of these words, as well as identify the definition and POS of the whole and parts.

airborne	claustrophobic	forerunner	jumpsuits	runoff	throwbacks
backfired	cobblestones	foresight	keepsakes	quicksand	wasteland
backfiring	comeback	forthcoming	lapdogs	sharpshooters	waterfowl
backlog	corkboard	gooseflesh	lockdown	sideswiped	waterlogged
backpedal	crisscross	greenhouse	manpower	sidetracked	whatnot
beeline (make a)	dovetail	groundskeeper	minefield	soundstage	whereabouts
blindsided	earpiece	halfhearted	minesweeping	stalemate	wherewithal
bloodlust	earshot (out of)	hardwood	mouthpiece	stockpiling	wholeheartedly
blowgun	easygoing	headdress	mudslides	stonecutters	windpipe
blowtorch	firebrand	headlamps	nosedive	storefront	wishbone
blueprints	firestorm	headpiece	noteworthy	sweetshop	
brainchild	flashback	heartsick	onslaught	switchblades	
brownouts	foothold	homecoming	parsnip	tailbone	
claustrophobia	footwork	hovercraft	pockmarked	tailspin	

Hyphenated

Since many open compounds become hyphenated when used as adjectives, one might expect this list to include mainly adjectives, and it does. You could have students discover this by giving them all the compound words and asking them to analyze structure and POS. They can also analyze the POS of words that make up the compounds, as well as brainstorm other words that have the same first or second word as the compounds listed.

all-consuming	cross-purposes	get-go	no-man's-land	self-appointed	white-hot
all-too-familiar	double-check	high-tech	on-camera	spanking-new	
back-stabbing	double-knot	home-brewed	one-way	staged-looking	
booby-trapped	drug-induced	last-ditch	razzle-dazzle	sure-footed	
camera-ready	fear-inducing	long-term	right-hand	tongue-tied	
close-cropped	full-scale	metal-studded	second-guess	well-to-do	

Multiple Endings, Same Base

This list can be used to help students review or study inflectional endings and other suffixes. For each set of two or more words, you can have students identify any or all of the following: the portion of the word that appears in all cases, the endings, the meanings, any spelling changes and pronunciation changes that distinguish the words, and the POS of each word. You could also ask them to write sentences or explain the meaning of one word in terms of the other. (e.g., "If you are *impulsive*, it means that you act on any *impulse* that you feel.) You could also have them categorize words by any of these criteria, for example, all the words in which an *e* was dropped to add an ending.; all the words that undergo a pronunciation change, and then see if they can draw any generalizations from the examples.

Spelling changes include the following, each with an example:

b --> p (absorbent --> absorption)   t --> s (divert --> diversion)   double consonant (consumes --> consummate)

k --> c (evoke --> evocative)   e --> i (unease --> uneasiness)   drop internal e (discreet --> discretion)

y --> i (arbitrary --> arbitrarily)   d --> s (extend --> extension)   drop final e (grime --> grimy)

t ---> c (potent --> potency)   d --> t (descending --> descent)

absorbent, absorption
arbitrary, arbitrarily
ascend, ascension
authoritative, authorized
backfired, backfiring
brutal, brutality, brute's, brutish
cavern, cavernous
claustrophobia, claustrophobic
clearance, clarifies, clarity
composed, composure
confines, confining
confronted, confrontation
conscious, consciousness
console, consolation
consumes, consumed, consummmate, consumption
contagion, contagious disease
contorts, contortions
cowed, cower
decomposing, decomposition
delusional, delusions
depicting, depiction
deplete, depleting
depressing, depression
descending, descent
detect, detection
deteriorated, deterioration
detonate, detonation
devise, devising
digesting, digestion
discreet, discretion
disorientation, disoriented
disposable, disposed
dissecting, dissection
diversion, divert
dogged, doggedly
ecstasy, ecstatically
electrocuted, electrocution
eludes, elusive
emanates, emanating
enhanced, enhancements

evasive, evasively
evocative, evoke
excess, excessive
exhale, exhalations
expose, exposed, exposure
extend, extension
fixated, fixation
flaw, flawless
formulation, formulated
fortifications, fortifying
frail, frailty
garrote, garroting
gene, genetic, genetically
grazed, grazing
grime, grimy
gritting, gritty
groom, grooms
harmonious, harmonize
illuminates, illumination
immersed, immersion
immobilized, immobilizing
immune, immunity
impotence, impotent
impulse, impulsive
incinerated, incineration
inexplicable, inexplicably
inflamed, inflammatory
inhabitants, inhabited
involuntarily, involuntary
inward, inwardly
justification, justify
lure, luring
manipulate, manipulative
mollified, mollify
mute, muted
obligated, obligatory, obliging
oblivion, oblivious
obsessions, obsessively
oppression, oppressors
optimism, optimistic
orient, orientation

plunk, plunking
potency, potent
preoccupation, preoccupied
project, projection
provocation, provocative
quench, unquenchable
radiant, radiating, radiation
rebellion, rebellious
reconcile, reconciliation
reflect, reflection
remedial, remedies
replica, replicate, replication
resistance, resistant
resolution, resolve
resonant, resonate
restraining, restraint
retaliate, retaliation
riveted, riveting
salvage, salvageable
sap, saplings
savor, savory
scarce, scarcity
scavenged, scavengers
sedated, sedative
sober, sobriety
speculate, speculation
spontaneity, spontaneously
squeamish, squeamishmess
stifles, stifling
stunned, stunner
subtle, subtleties
sustained, sustaining
swathe, swathed
toxic, toxicity
traitor, traitorous
transformation, transformed
unease, uneasiness
unraveled, unraveling
validation, validity
vapor, vaporized
vengeance, vengeful